ASSISTANCE LEAGUE OF NORMAN, OKLAHOMA

Tailgates to Tea Parties

Where Southern Comforts Meet Western Sizzle

Tailgates to Tea Parties

Published by Assistance League® of Norman

Copyright © 2005
Assistance League® of Norman
809 Wall Street
Norman, Oklahoma 73069

This cookbook is a collection of favorite recipes,
which are not necessarily original recipes.

Thanks to Leaf it to Us florist in Moore,
Oklahoma, for the floral arrangements.
Our stylist was Jeri Saliba.

Photography:
pages 11 and 55 © Shevaun Williams;
pages 77 and 129 © Konrad Eek;
pages 29, 119, and 151 © Simon Hurst

Library of Congress Control Number: 2004094624

ISBN: 0-9753606-0-4

Edited, Designed, and Manufactured by
Favorite Recipes® Press
An Imprint of **FRP**
P.O. Box 305142, Nashville, Tennessee 37230
800-358-0560

Art Director: Steve Newman
Book Design: Dave Malone
Project Manager: Nicki Pendleton Wood
Managing Editor: Mary Cummings

Manufactured in the United States of America
First Printing 2005 10,000 copies

Proceeds from *Tailgates to Tea Parties* will be used
to support the philanthropic projects of Assistance
League® of Norman.

2

Epigraph

This book is a lasting symbol of our
organization and will bring our
membership's culinary talents to our
community and beyond.

Mission Statement

Assistance League® of Norman is a nonprofit
philanthropic volunteer organization dedicated
to creating and funding service projects that enrich
the lives of the Norman community while fostering
bonds of friendship and respect among its members.

Foreword

Every family treasures the recipes that have been
prepared and handed down by those who have
nourished and comforted its members.
A community does as well.

That is why this Assistance League® of Norman
Cookbook will be treasured by members
of the Norman community for years to come.
The members of the Assistance League
of Norman are the nurturers and comforters
of our community.

These dedicated volunteers reach out to assault
victims, children, the homeless, arts and education
programs, senior citizens, and other members
of our community in need of nurture and comfort.
They provide a sense of family for our community.

This cookbook, compiled of recipes from ALN
members, is a special gift to our common family—
the Norman community. These dishes we lovingly
prepare for our own families and friends will remind
us of the love and care the authors provide those
in need in our beloved community of Norman,
Oklahoma. We thank them for their service and
for sharing their favorite recipes.

Molly Shi Boren
Norman, Oklahoma

Cookbook Committees

2001-2003 Cookbook Committee
Jerrie Anderson
Donna Buwick
Pam Clinton
Mary Carol Gilbert
Samia Harroz
Sandra Hook
Donna Hughes
Linda Leemaster
Carrie Mitchell
Gail Mullins
Ann Niemeyer
Helen Parker
Kirsten Plusquellec
Carolyn Rodgers
Jeri Saliba
Lexa Shafer

2003-2005 Cookbook Committee
Mary Carol Gilbert
Donna Hughes
Linda Leemaster
Carrie Mitchell
Helen Parker
Jeri Saliba
Lexa Shafer
Carol Toperzer
Judy Travis
JoAnne Zmud

Contents

6

Contents

7

Contents

Preface

Assistance League® of Norman (ALN)
is one of 106 chapters of National
Assistance League®, a nonprofit,
nonpolitical, nonsectarian organization.
ALN was founded in 1970 and was
the 56th chapter chartered by National
Assistance League on May 2, 1974,
with 58 active members. Today, ALN has
almost 600 members within five membership
classifications. Members bring a wealth
of skills to the chapter's philanthropic projects
and activities through their community
volunteer experience and professional careers as
attorneys, teachers, accountants, doctors,
designers, business owners, etc.

Our members have contributed more than
500,000 hours of community service since 1970.
Through the years, all proceeds of Assistance
League fund-raising activities, combined with
donations from local foundations, businesses, and
individuals, have been returned to the community
through ALN philanthropic projects. Assistance
League of Norman has never applied for United
Way® funding. Assistance League members
serve the Norman area by giving their time and
financial support to eight philanthropic projects.

ASK® (Assault Survivor Kits)—Assault victims have their clothes held as evidence when they are treated at the local hospital. This project provides clothing and other personal items to help the victim leave more comfortably.

Book of My Own—Children who receive clothing through OPERATION SCHOOL BELL® are also given the opportunity to select a book of their choice to take home.

Care Kits—Grooming kits are supplied to women and children temporarily residing in a women's shelter due to abuse. Personal and household items are also provided when the women leave the shelter to move into their own homes. Kits are also given to independent-living high school students.

Kindergarten Round-Up—Each spring, ALN volunteers assist school personnel by conducting the pre-enrollment of over 500 children for kindergarten and first grade.

May Fair Arts Festival—An annual three-day art festival featuring more than 70 artists and craftspeople. It is enjoyed by more than 50,000 people each year. Everyone can enjoy fine art, children's art activities, a student art show, restaurant specialties, entertainment, and special events. In addition, each year, a "Celebrated Artist" is highlighted for the benefit of all in attendance.

OPERATION SCHOOL BELL® (OSB)—OSB provides new clothing, shoes, and grooming kits to eligible children in pre-kindergarten through grade 12 in Norman and Little Axe public school systems. They are referred to OSB by school officials. Each year, members help more than 1,200 students select new clothing in a store-like atmosphere.

Seniors R&R—Each month, chapter members provide recreation and companionship to those in the participating facility. The members direct activities such as dancing, themed parties, and bingo with the seniors, while providing prizes and serving refreshments.

TAILGATES TO TEA PARTIES

Chapter Recipes

Appetizers & Beverages

Hot Corn Dip

1 (11-ounce) can Mexican-style corn
2 cups (8 ounces) shredded
Monterey Jack cheese
$^1/_2$ cup (2 ounces) grated Parmesan cheese
1 cup mayonnaise
1 (4-ounce) can black olives
2 (4-ounce) cans green chiles
1 (2-ounce) jar pimento, drained, diced
Dash of garlic salt
Dash of Tabasco sauce

Combine the corn, Monterey Jack cheese, Parmesan cheese, mayonnaise, olives, green chiles, pimento, garlic salt and Tabasco sauce in a bowl and mix well. Spoon into a greased baking dish. Bake, uncovered, at 350 degrees for 30 minutes. Serve with corn chips. Makes 15 servings.

Note: *You may mix this early in the day and then bake right before serving. The scoop-shaped corn chips work really well with this dip.*

Hot Mushroom Dip

1 pound mushrooms, minced
6 tablespoons butter
1 tablespoon lemon juice
2 tablespoons minced onion
2 cups sour cream
2 teaspoons chicken bouillon granules or
2 chicken bouillon cubes, dissolved
Salt and pepper to taste
2 tablespoons butter, softened
2 tablespoons flour

Cook the mushrooms with 6 tablespoons butter and lemon juice in a large skillet for 10 minutes. Stir in the onion, sour cream, bouillon, salt and pepper. Combine 2 tablespoons butter and the flour in a small bowl and mix to a paste consistency; add to the mushroom mixture. Cook until thickened, stirring constantly. Remove to a chafing dish. Serve hot with chips, crackers or fresh raw vegetables. Makes 20 servings.

Note: *If you have any dip left over, it's delicious used as a sauce for pork tenderloin or other meats.*

Hot Onion Soufflé

2 tablespoons butter or margarine
3 large Vidalia onions, chopped (3 to 4 cups)
24 ounces cream cheese, softened
2 cups (8 ounces) grated Parmesan cheese
1/4 cup mayonnaise

Heat the butter in a skillet; add the onions and sauté over medium-high heat until tender. Add the cream cheese, Parmesan cheese and mayonnaise to the onions and mix well. Spoon into a greased 2-quart soufflé dish. Bake at 425 degrees for 15 minutes or until golden brown. Serve with crackers. Makes 15 to 20 servings.

Note: *Nothing beats the taste of fresh Vidalia onions, but if you are pressed for time, you may substitute two 10-ounce packages of frozen chopped onions.*

There are many different types of onions available in today's markets. Many sweet onions have been developed to meet the demand, and one type or another is available almost year-round. Some popular sweet onions are cipollini, Walla Walla, Vidalia, SpringSweets, 1015 SuperSweets, Sweet Imperial, AmeriSweet, Maui, OSO Sweets, and Rio Sweets. Storage onions are available year-round and include yellow and white globe, Bermuda, Spanish, and purple or red. These types have a more pungent taste than their sweet relatives.

Festive Hot Salmon Dip

1 (8-ounce) package cream cheese, softened
1/2 cup mayonnaise
1 tablespoon prepared horseradish
1 teaspoon dill weed
1 teaspoon Worcestershire sauce
1 (6-ounce) can salmon, drained
1/4 cup chopped red bell pepper
1/4 cup chopped green onions

Combine the cream cheese and mayonnaise in a bowl and mix well. Stir in the horseradish, dill weed and Worcestershire sauce. Add the salmon, bell pepper and green onions and mix well. Spread the mixture evenly in a 9-inch round or 9×9-inch square baking dish. Bake at 375 degrees for 20 to 25 minutes or until heated through. Serve on toasted party bread. Makes 6 to 10 servings.

Island Crab Dip

1 cup mayonnaise
1 cup sour cream
1 cup shredded coconut
6 ounces crab meat
1/2 cup chopped onion
2 tablespoons chopped fresh parsley
1 teaspoon curry powder
Salt and pepper to taste

Combine the mayonnaise, sour cream, coconut, crab meat, onion, parsley, curry powder, salt and pepper in a bowl and mix well. Chill until serving time. Serve the dip in a hollowed-out pineapple with slices of the pineapple and crackers on the side. Makes 8 to 12 servings.

Note: *The secret to this delicious dip is the coconut. This was a popular dish at May Fair's "Opening Night."*

Appetizers & Beverages

Crab Mousse

6 ounces cream cheese
1 (10-ounce) can cream of mushroom soup
1 small onion, grated
1 envelope unflavored gelatin
$^{1}/_{4}$ cup cold water
1 cup finely chopped celery
6 ounces fresh or canned crab meat, drained,
flaked (rinse canned crab meat)
1 cup mayonnaise
1 tablespoon Worcestershire sauce
$^{1}/_{4}$ teaspoon Tabasco sauce

Heat the cream cheese, soup and onion in a double boiler over hot simmering water until smooth and creamy. Soften the gelatin in the water. Cook over low heat until the gelatin is completely dissolved, stirring constantly. Add the gelatin and celery to the double boiler and mix well. Stir in the crab meat, mayonnaise, Worcestershire sauce and Tabasco sauce. Pour into a $4^{1}/_{2}$-cup mold coated with nonstick cooking spray. Chill for 3 to 10 hours. Unmold onto a serving plate. Serve with crackers or toasted party bread. Makes 10 to 12 servings.

Note: *For a crab-shrimp mousse, use 1 can crab meat and 1 can shrimp. For a big party, double the recipe and use a bundt pan for the mold.*

Dill Dip for Vegetables

1 cup mayonnaise
1 cup sour cream
1 tablespoon minced onion
3 tablespoons parsley
1 tablespoon chives
$1^{1}/_{3}$ teaspoons seasoned salt
$1^{1}/_{2}$ teaspoons dill weed

Combine the mayonnaise, sour cream, onion, parsley, chives, seasoned salt and dill weed in a bowl and mix well. Chill for several hours before serving. Serve with fresh vegetables or crackers. Makes 10 to 12 servings.

Note: *This dip also makes a great topping for baked potatoes.*

Nesselrode Mousse

12 ounces cream cheese, softened
1/2 cup (1 stick) butter, softened
1/2 cup sour cream
1/2 cup sugar
1 envelope unflavored gelatin
1/4 cup cold water
1/2 cup golden raisins
1/2 cup slivered almonds, toasted
Grated zest of 2 lemons

Combine the cream cheese, butter and sour cream in a bowl and beat until smooth. Stir in the sugar. Soften the gelatin in the water in a double boiler. Cook over simmering water until the gelatin is completely dissolved, stirring constantly. Add to the cream cheese mixture and mix well. Stir in the raisins, almonds and lemon zest. Pour into a greased 1-quart mold. Chill for 8 to 10 hours. Serve with crackers. Makes 20 to 25 servings.

Rosalynn Carter's Cheese Ring

4 cups (1 pound) shredded sharp Cheddar cheese
1 cup chopped pecans
1 cup mayonnaise
1 small onion, minced
1/2 teaspoon cayenne pepper
2 cups strawberry preserves

Combine the cheese, pecans, mayonnaise, onion and cayenne pepper in a bowl and mix well. Spoon the mixture into a greased ring mold, pressing firmly. Chill for 8 to 10 hours. Unmold onto a serving plate. Spoon the preserves into the center of the ring. Serve with butter crackers. Makes 20 to 25 servings.

Note: *This recipe originated with Henry Haller, who was White House chef to several First Families, including the Carters. Another version of this cheese ring increases the amount of mayonnaise to 2 cups, adds 1 pressed garlic clove and 1/2 teaspoon Tabasco sauce, and reduces the amount of preserves to 1 cup. Try varying the type of preserves used in the center.*

Southwest Cheese Bread

1/2 cup (1 stick) butter
Garlic salt to taste
1 (4-ounce) can green chiles, drained, chopped
1 cup (4 ounces) shredded
Monterey Jack cheese
1/2 cup mayonnaise
1 loaf French bread, cut in half lengthwise

Melt the butter in a saucepan. Stir in the garlic salt and green chiles. Combine the cheese and mayonnaise in a small bowl and mix well. Spread the butter mixture on both lengths of the bread. Spread with the cheese mixture. Bake on a baking sheet at 400 degrees for 20 minutes. Slice into serving-size pieces. Makes 8 to 12 servings.

Creamy Chicken and Jalapeño Nachos

1 whole chicken breast, cooked, boned and chopped
12 ounces cream cheese, softened
2 jalapeño chiles, seeded, minced
3 tablespoons chopped red onion
2 garlic cloves, minced
1 teaspoon each cumin and chili powder
1 1/2 cups (6 ounces) shredded
Monterey Jack cheese
Salt and pepper to taste
6 pita bread rounds, each separated into 2 rounds

Combine the chicken, cream cheese, jalapeño chiles, onion, garlic, cumin, chili powder and Monterey Jack cheese in a large mixing bowl and beat until smooth. Add salt and pepper. Spread the filling generously on each pita bread round. Cut each round into 6 wedges. Bake on a baking sheet at 375 degrees for 5 to 7 minutes or until the filling is puffed and bubbly. Serve immediately. Makes 72 servings.

Note: *The nachos may be prepared and frozen before baking.*

Two-Cheese Spread

1 (8-ounce) package cream cheese, softened
1/2 cup sour cream
1 envelope Italian-style dressing mix
1 cup (4 ounces) shredded Cheddar cheese

Beat the cream cheese in a mixing bowl at medium speed until fluffy. Add the sour cream and dressing mix and beat until well blended. Stir in the Cheddar cheese, reserving 1 tablespoon cheese. Spoon the spread into a serving dish and sprinkle with the reserved cheese. Serve with crackers. Makes 10 to 12 servings.

Avocado and Basil Bruschetta

2 ripe avocados, peeled, sliced or chopped
1 tablespoon lemon juice
2 teaspoons extra-virgin olive oil
1 small garlic clove, peeled
3/4 cup parsley leaves
3/4 cup basil leaves
1/3 cup extra-virgin olive oil
1 1/2 teaspoons red wine vinegar
1 loaf French bread
2 red tomatoes, chopped
2 yellow tomatoes, chopped

Toss the avocados with the lemon juice and 2 teaspoons olive oil in a medium bowl. Purée the garlic, parsley, basil, 1/3 cup olive oil and vinegar in a blender or food processor fitted with a metal blade. Cut the bread into slices and toast. Spread the basil mixture on each slice and top with the avocados and tomatoes. Makes 20 pieces.

Avocados

Don't wait for an avocado to ripen. Instead, simply prick the skin in a couple of places and then microwave it on High for up to one minute. It is then ready to use immediately.

Tortilla Roll-Ups

12 to 15 (8-inch) flour tortillas
Cream Cheese Filling
Spinach Filling

Spread half the tortillas with Cream Cheese Filling and half with Spinach Filling. Roll up the tortillas and wrap each in plastic wrap. Chill for at least 3 hours. Cut each roll diagonally into 8 or 10 slices. Makes 100 to 150 servings.

Cream Cheese Filling

2 (8-ounce) packages cream cheese, softened
1 envelope ranch salad dressing mix
4 green onions, chopped
1 (4-ounce) can diced green chiles, drained
1 (4-ounce) jar diced pimentos, drained
1/3 cup chopped black olives

Combine the cream cheese and dressing mix in a mixing bowl and beat until fluffy. Stir in the green onions, green chiles, pimentos and olives. Makes 2 cups.

Spinach Filling

1 cup mayonnaise
1 cup sour cream
1 envelope ranch salad dressing mix
2 (10-ounce) packages frozen chopped spinach, thawed, squeezed dry
1/3 cup bacon bits

Combine the mayonnaise, sour cream, dressing mix, spinach and bacon bits in a bowl and mix well. Makes 3 cups.

Vegetable Bars

2 (8-count) cans crescent rolls
2 (8-ounce) packages cream cheese, softened
3/4 cup mayonnaise
1/2 cup sour cream
1 envelope ranch salad dressing mix
3/4 cup each of assorted toppings
(chopped broccoli, tomatoes, green onions,
green or black olives, bell pepper, grated
cheese or carrots)

Unroll the crescent roll dough. Spread out dough on a baking sheet coated with nonstick cooking spray. Press perforations in the dough to seal. Bake at 350 degrees for 7 to 8 minutes or until brown. Let stand until cool. Combine the cream cheese, mayonnaise, sour cream and dressing mix in a bowl and mix well. Spread over the crust. Combine your choice of toppings and sprinkle over the cream cheese layer. Cover with plastic wrap and press the toppings into the cream cheese mixture. Chill for 3 to 4 hours. Cut into bars. Makes 24 servings.

Asparagus Wraps

24 fresh asparagus spears
1 cup mayonnaise-type salad dressing
1 bunch green onions, minced
1 loaf thin-sliced sandwich bread,
crusts trimmed

Steam the asparagus for 6 minutes. Plunge the asparagus into cold water to stop the cooking process. Drain and dry well. Combine the salad dressing and green onions in a bowl. Roll the bread slices flat with a rolling pin. Spread each slice with the onion mixture; top with an asparagus spear. Roll up the bread around the asparagus. Place seam side down on a greased baking sheet. Broil for 2 to 3 minutes or until brown on top. Serve immediately. Makes 24 servings.

Salsa Ranchera

1 medium white onion, quartered
3 pounds medium tomatoes, cored
$^{1}/_{2}$ cup olive oil
1 fresh serrano chile, chopped, including seeds
$^{1}/_{2}$ cup chopped fresh cilantro
3 tablespoons red wine vinegar
Salt to taste

Combine 2 onion quarters and 2 pounds of the tomatoes in a small roasting pan. Drizzle with $^{1}/_{4}$ cup of the olive oil. Place the remaining 1 pound tomatoes in a small baking dish and drizzle with the remaining $^{1}/_{4}$ cup olive oil. Place the roasting pan in the upper third of the oven and the baking dish in the lower third of the oven. Roast at 400 degrees for 45 minutes. Switch the positions of the pan and baking dish and roast for 45 minutes longer. Remove the pan. Roast the tomatoes in the baking dish for about 30 minutes longer or until blackened.

Place all the roasted tomatoes and onions in a food processor, discarding the cooking liquid. Pulse until coarsely chopped. Chop the remaining 2 onion quarters; add with the serrano chile, cilantro and vinegar to the tomato mixture. Season with salt. Chill for at least 8 hours. Bring the salsa to room temperature before serving. Serve with corn tortilla chips. Makes 4 cups.

Note: *The salsa will keep well, covered and chilled, for 3 days.*

As a rule of thumb, the longer and thinner the pepper, the hotter the taste. To lower the heat of peppers, remove the seeds and ribs before adding to the dish.

Fresh Tomato Salsa

3 medium tomatoes, diced
1/4 cup chopped green chiles, rinsed, drained
1/4 cup diced red onion
1/4 cup diced green bell pepper
2 tablespoons chopped fresh parsley
1 tablespoon lime juice
1/4 teaspoon cumin
1/4 teaspoon hot red pepper sauce
1/4 teaspoon salt
1/4 teaspoon garlic powder

Combine the tomatoes, green chiles, onion, bell pepper, parsley, lime juice, cumin, hot sauce, salt and garlic powder in a bowl and mix well. Let stand for 15 minutes. Serve with unsalted tortilla chips or with grilled chicken or fish. Makes 3 cups.

Red River Caviar

3 (16-ounce) cans black-eyed peas, drained
1 large green bell pepper, diced
1 cup diced jalapeño chiles or green chiles
1/4 cup diced pimento
1 teaspoon minced garlic
1 (8-ounce) bottle Italian dressing

Combine the black-eyed peas, bell pepper, jalapeño chiles, pimento, garlic and Italian dressing in a bowl and mix well. Chill for 8 to 10 hours. Serve with chips. Makes 10 to 12 servings.

Note: *While this is delicious as a dip, it's also great served as a cold salad alongside burgers or other grilled meats.*

Appetizers & Beverages

Tomatoes should never be stored in the refrigerator. The cold will hurt both the texture and the flavor.

Crunch Punch

3 (3-ounce) packages gelatin (any flavor)
9 cups boiling water
4 cups sugar
4 cups water
1 (16-ounce) bottle lemon juice
2 (46-ounce) cans pineapple juice
6 large bottles ginger ale

Dissolve the gelatin in the boiling water in a large container. Mix the sugar with 4 cups water in a saucepan. Boil until the sugar is dissolved. Add to the gelatin. Cool slightly. Stir in the lemon juice and pineapple juice. Let stand until cool. Freeze the punch in sealable plastic freezer bags. Thaw the punch partially in the microwave. Pour into a punch bowl and add enough of the ginger ale to dilute the punch. Makes 50 servings.

Note: *Be careful not to dilute this punch too much. There should still be bits of shaved ice throughout. Another, perhaps easier, way to freeze the punch is in ice cube trays. Once the cubes are frozen, remove them to resealable plastic bags. Add the cubes directly to the punch bowl and add the ginger ale.*

Beta House Punch

3 cups sugar
6 cups water
1 (12-ounce) can frozen orange
juice concentrate, thawed
1 (6-ounce) can frozen lemon
juice concentrate, thawed
1 (46-ounce) can pineapple juice
4 bananas
5 quarts ginger ale, chilled
4 bottles Champagne, chilled

Mix the sugar and water in a saucepan. Boil until the sugar is dissolved. Stir in the orange juice, lemon juice and pineapple juice. Combine the bananas and a small amount of the juice mixture in a blender or food processor and blend well. Pour into a freezer container and freeze. Refrigerate the remaining juice mixture.

Thaw the banana mixture partially and pour into a punch bowl. Add the remaining juice mixture, ginger ale and Champagne. Makes 40 servings.

Salem College Tea

8 to 12 whole cloves
2 cinnamon sticks
4 sprigs of fresh mint (optional)
3 quarts water
14 tea bags
Juice of 8 lemons
Juice of 6 oranges
1 (46-ounce) can pineapple juice
2 cups sugar

Combine the cloves, cinnamon sticks, mint and water in a saucepan. Bring to a boil and simmer for 10 to 15 minutes. Remove from the heat. Add the tea bags and let steep for 10 to 15 minutes. Strain the punch, discarding the solids. Add the lemon juice, orange juice, pineapple juice and sugar to the hot tea and stir until the sugar is dissolved. Serve hot or cold. Makes 12 to 16 servings.

Note: *If the tea is too sweet for your taste, try making the recipe with half the amount of sugar.*

Frozen Margarita Punch

4 (12-ounce) cans frozen limeade
concentrate, thawed
3 quarts water
3 cups Cointreau
3 cups gold tequila
4 liters lemon-lime soda, chilled

Combine the limeade, water, Cointreau and tequila in a freezer container. Freeze for at least 8 hours. Thaw for 30 minutes before serving. Break into chunks and place in a punch bowl. Stir in the lemon-lime soda. Serve immediately. Makes 30 servings.

Note: *This punch keeps well in the freezer for up to 2 months.*

The Birth of the Margarita

The year was 1947. An American couple, Mr. and Mrs. Sames, was spending the Christmas holiday at their vacation home in Acapulco, where they entertained frequently. Mrs. Sames was particularly fond of a drink favored by the locals: tequila with lime juice. She also enjoyed Cointreau, a liqueur imported from France. During one particularly festive evening, she began experimenting with her two favorite drinks and soon poured a concoction mixed from equal parts tequila, Cointreau, and fresh lime juice over ice. The Drink, as it came to be known, was the hit of the season. The following year, the Sameses returned. On Christmas Eve, Mr. Sames presented his wife with long-stemmed crystal glasses having shallow, flat bowls, perfect for serving The Drink. Etched into each glass was the name of his beloved wife: Margarita. The rest is history.

Fresh Peach Daiquiris

2 cups sliced peeled fresh peaches
1 (6-ounce) can frozen lemonade
concentrate, thawed
1/2 cup light rum
1/4 cup 151-proof rum
1/4 cup sugar or less

Combine the peaches, lemonade, light rum, dark rum and sugar in a blender. Fill with ice and process until smooth. Makes 4 to 6 servings.

Note: *Adjust the amount of sugar in this recipe according to the sweetness of the peaches.*

Raspberry Bellini

1 bag frozen unsweetened raspberries, thawed
2 tablespoons sugar
1 (750-milliliter) bottle brut
Champagne, chilled

Combine the raspberries and sugar in a food processor or blender and process until puréed. Strain the purée through a sieve, discarding the seeds. Place 1 tablespoon of raspberry purée in each of 6 Champagne flutes. Fill with the Champagne and stir gently. Makes 6 servings.

Milk Punch

1 quart brandy
1 quart Kahlúa
Milk

Combine the brandy and Kahlúa in a 1-gallon milk jug. Fill to the top with milk. Shake well before serving. Makes 25 to 30 servings.

Iced Hazelnut Coffee

12 cups hot strong coffee
3/4 cup ground hazelnuts
1 large cinnamon stick

Steep the coffee, hazelnuts and cinnamon stick in a saucepan until the coffee reaches room temperature. Pour the coffee through a sieve lined with a 3/4-inch thickness of cheesecloth. Gather the cheesecloth with the hazelnuts enclosed and squeeze over the coffee. Serve chilled over crushed ice. Makes 12 servings.

Mexican Coffee

4 ounces tequila
4 ounces Kahlúa
24 ounces semisweet chocolate, grated
4 cups hot strong coffee
Whipped cream
Ground cinnamon

Divide the tequila, Kahlúa and chocolate equally into the 4 cups coffee. Top each with a dollop of whipped cream and a sprinkle of cinnamon. Makes 4 servings.

Coffee Float

2/3 cup heavy cream
4 teaspoons honey
8 scoops coffee ice cream
1 1/2 cups hot strong coffee
Grated dark chocolate

Beat the cream and honey in a mixing bowl and beat until stiff peaks form. Place 2 scoops of the ice cream in each of 4 tall-stemmed glasses. Pour the coffee over the ice cream, dividing evenly among the 4 servings. Top each with a dollop of the honey whipped cream and a sprinkling of grated chocolate. Makes 4 servings.

Chapter Recipes

Soups & Salads

Kansas City Steak Soup

1 pound ground round
2 small white onions, chopped
3 ribs celery, chopped
2 carrots, diced
1 (15-ounce) can diced tomatoes
1 (10-ounce) package frozen mixed vegetables
3 cups water
3 beef bouillon cubes
1 tablespoon each garlic salt and MSG
1 teaspoon pepper
2 tablespoons butter
4 to 6 tablespoons flour
1 (10-ounce) can beef broth

Brown the ground round in a skillet, stirring until crumbly; drain. Combine the beef, onions, celery, carrots, tomatoes, mixed vegetables, water, bouillon cubes, garlic salt, MSG and pepper in a slow cooker. Cook on High for 4 hours or on Low for 8 hours. Heat the butter in a saucepan; add the flour and cook for 2 minutes, stirring constantly. Stir in the broth. Cook until the broth mixture thickens. Add the broth mixture to the slow cooker and stir well. Cook on High until the soup thickens slightly.
Makes 8 to 12 servings.

Hearty Cabbage Soup

1 pound ground beef
6 cups water
2 (6-ounce) cans tomato paste
1/2 medium head cabbage, chopped
1 large onion, sliced
4 allspice berries, or 1/8 teaspoon ground allspice
3 tablespoons sugar (optional)
2 tablespoons Worcestershire sauce
1 tablespoon salt
3 peppercorns
1 bay leaf

Brown the beef in a skillet, stirring until crumbly; drain. Combine the beef, water, tomato paste, cabbage, onion, allspice berries, sugar, Worcestershire sauce, salt, peppercorns and bay leaf in a soup pot. Bring to a boil. Reduce the heat and simmer for 1 hour. Discard the bay leaf before serving. Makes 8 servings.

Note: *This soup tastes even better the second day.*

Cream of Chestnut Soup

1 large onion, chopped
$1/2$ cup chopped celery
3 tablespoons butter
1 bay leaf
$1/2$ teaspoon coriander
1 jar peeled chestnuts (3 cups)
6 cups unsalted chicken stock
$1^1/2$ cups heavy cream
$1/4$ cup madeira
2 teaspoons salt, or to taste
1 teaspoon white pepper, or to taste
Chopped fresh parsley

Sauté the onion and celery in the butter in a soup pot until tender and translucent, stirring frequently. Add the bay leaf and coriander. Cook for 1 minute, stirring constantly. Add the chestnuts and stock. Bring to a boil. Reduce the heat and simmer for 45 minutes or until the chestnuts begin to crumble, stirring constantly. Remove from the heat and let stand until the soup is room temperature.

Strain the soup through a large sieve over a bowl. Discard the bay leaf. Combine $1/2$ of the solids with 1 cup of the liquid in a food processor or blender and process until smooth, adding more liquid as needed to make a smooth consistency. Pour the puréed soup into a clean soup pot. Purée the remaining $1/2$ of the solids and liquid. Add to the soup pot. Chill until serving time or up to several days. Reheat the soup over low heat for 1 hour before serving. Stir in the cream, madeira, salt and white pepper. Garnish with chopped fresh parsley. Makes 8 servings.

Garnishing Your Soup

Garnishes add contrasting flavor and texture to a soup and enhance its visual appeal. A few suggestions: chopped bell peppers, crème fraîche, shredded cheese, crisp bacon bits, toasted sesame seeds, chopped fresh herbs, thinly sliced fruit, capers, chopped nuts, peppercorns, avocado slices, or crumbled corn chips. Try squeezing a ribbon or drops of sour cream through a plastic condiment squeeze bottle over the soup; then drag a wooden pick through the sour cream to create a swirled effect.

Chicken Noodle Soup

The chicken stock:

3 pounds boneless skinless chicken breasts

4 celery rib tops (leaves)

2 carrots, chopped

1 small onion, chopped

2 teaspoons salt

1 teaspoon pepper

$4^{1}/2$ cups (or more) water

For the chicken stock, combine the chicken, celery tops, carrots, onion, salt, pepper and water in a soup pot. Bring to a boil and skim off the foam. Reduce the heat and simmer for 45 minutes or until the chicken is tender. Remove the chicken and let cool. Cut the chicken into large or small pieces, as desired. Strain the stock, discarding the vegetables.

The soup:

$^{1}/4$ cup chopped onion

1 teaspoon minced garlic

2 tablespoons butter

2 medium ribs celery, sliced ($1^{1}/2$ cups)

2 cans chicken broth

2 medium carrots, sliced ($1^{1}/2$ cups)

1 tablespoon Italian seasoning

$^{1}/2$ teaspoon salt

$^{1}/2$ teaspoon pepper

1 package noodles

For the soup, sauté the onion and garlic in the butter in a soup pot until the onion is tender. Add the celery. Cook until tender. Add the stock, chicken, broth, carrots, Italian seasoning, salt and pepper. Bring to a boil. Reduce the heat and simmer for 30 minutes or until the carrots are tender. Stir in the noodles. Simmer until the noodles are tender. Makes 8 to 10 servings.

Note: *If you would like to have this soup on hand in your freezer, prepare as above, but do not add the noodles. Cook the noodles in the soup after defrosting.*

Salty Soup

If you have added too much salt to your stock or soup, add a few potato slices and simmer for a few minutes. Repeat if necessary with fresh potato slices until the saltiness is sufficiently reduced.

Chicken Tortellini Stew

The chicken stock:

4 to 6 chicken breasts

1 can Italian-seasoned chicken broth

1 can chicken broth

1 rib celery, chopped

1 carrot, chopped

1 slice onion, chopped

1 or 2 garlic cloves, chopped

1 teaspoon oregano

1 teaspoon basil

2 teaspoons celery salt

For the chicken stock, combine the chicken, broths, celery, carrot, onion, garlic, oregano, basil and celery salt in a soup pot. Bring to a boil. Reduce the heat and simmer for 45 minutes or until the chicken is tender. Remove the chicken and let cool. Cube the chicken.

The stew:

2 ribs celery, chopped

1 red bell pepper, chopped

1 green bell pepper, chopped

4 carrots, sliced

4 ounces fresh green beans, trimmed, cut into 1-inch lengths

1 pound spinach, stems removed, chopped

8 ounces frozen peas

1 or 2 zucchini, halved, sliced

1 package refrigerator cheese tortellini

For the stew, add the celery, bell peppers, carrots, green beans, spinach, peas and zucchini to the chicken stock. Bring to a boil. Reduce the heat and simmer for 15 minutes. Add the tortellini. Simmer for 15 minutes. Stir in the cubed chicken. Simmer for 5 minutes longer. Makes 8 servings.

Note: *Be sure to use a large enough soup pot for this soup, at least a 5-quart size. If you find the soup is a little thick for the amount of vegetables, add some extra canned broth.*

Soups & Salads

Texas Tortilla Soup

1 pound chicken breasts, chopped
$^1/_2$ cup vegetable oil
$^1/_4$ cup ($^1/_2$ stick) butter
1 large onion, chopped
1 jalapeño chile, seeded, chopped
4 garlic cloves, minced
2 large carrots, diced
6 ribs celery, diced
1 teaspoon cumin
1 teaspoon chili powder
1 teaspoon salt
1 teaspoon lemon pepper
1 tablespoon hot red pepper sauce
$^1/_2$ cup flour
1 (14-ounce) can tomatoes, or
1$^1/_2$ (10-ounce) cans tomatoes with
green chiles
4 cans chicken broth
8 corn tortillas, cut into strips
3 avocados, diced
1 cup (4 ounces) shredded cheese
1 cup sour cream

Sauté the chicken in the oil in a soup pot; drain. Add the butter, onion, jalapeño chile, garlic, carrots and celery. Sauté for 5 minutes. Stir in the cumin, chili powder, salt, lemon pepper, hot sauce and flour. Add the tomatoes and broth. Bring to a boil. Reduce the heat and simmer for 1 hour, stirring occasionally. Broil the tortilla strips until crisp. Ladle the soup into bowls and top with the tortilla strips, avocados, cheese and sour cream. Makes 8 servings.

New England Clam Chowder

8 slices bacon, coarsely chopped
4 cups finely chopped onions
8 cups diced potatoes
2 cups water
4 teaspoons salt
Dash of pepper
4 pints shucked fresh clams, or
8 (11-ounce) cans minced or whole clams
8 cups half-and-half
1/2 cup (1 stick) butter or margarine
2 cups (8 ounces) shredded cheese (optional)

Cook the bacon in a large kettle until almost crisp. Add the onions. Cook for 5 minutes. Add the potatoes, water, salt and pepper. Cook, uncovered, for 15 minutes or until the potatoes are tender. Drain the clams, reserving the liquid, and chop coarsely. Add the clams, 2 cups clam liquid, half-and-half and butter. Cook over low heat for 3 minutes or just until hot and not boiling. Stir in the cheese. Makes 16 servings.

Baked Potato Soup

2/3 cup butter
2/3 cup flour
7 cups milk
4 large potatoes, baked, cooled, peeled, cubed
4 green onions, sliced
12 slices bacon, crisp-cooked, crumbled
1 1/4 cups (5 ounces) shredded Cheddar cheese
1 cup sour cream
3/4 teaspoon salt
1/2 teaspoon pepper

Melt the butter in a soup kettle or Dutch oven. Add the flour and stir until smooth. Stir in the milk gradually. Cook until thickened, stirring constantly. Add the potatoes and green onions. Bring to a boil, stirring constantly. Reduce the heat and simmer for 10 minutes. Add the bacon, cheese, sour cream, salt and pepper. Cook until the cheese is melted, stirring constantly. Serve immediately. Makes 8 to 10 servings.

Note: *This soup may be partially prepared in advance. After the potatoes and onions are cooked, let the soup cool. Chill until serving time. Reheat the soup, adding the bacon and remaining ingredients just before serving.*

Grilled Corn and Chipotle Soup

6 medium ears of corn, grilled
1/4 cup diced red onion
2 or 3 chipotle chiles
Dash of white pepper
Dash of cumin
2 cups water
4 cups heavy cream
Tortillas, cut into wedges and fried
Corn Relish

Remove the grilled corn kernels from the cobs with a sharp knife. Reserve 1/4 of the kernels for the Corn Relish. Combine 1/2 of the corn kernels, the onion, chipotle chiles, white pepper, cumin and 1 cup of the water in a food processor or blender and pulse until a coarse paste consistency. Add more of the water if necessary to blend, leaving some chunks of corn in the mixture. Combine the corn mixture, cream and any remaining water in a soup pot. Bring to a boil. Reduce the heat and simmer for 15 to 20 minutes or until the soup has thickened and reduced by about 1/2. Garnish each serving with a crispy tortilla wedge and a dollop of Corn Relish. Makes 4 to 8 servings.

Corn Relish

Grilled corn (reserved from
Grilled Corn and Chipotle Soup)
1 tablespoon diced green bell pepper
1 tablespoon diced red bell pepper
1/8 teaspoon minced fresh jalapeño chile
3 tablespoons white wine vinegar
1 teaspoon honey
Salt to taste

Combine the grilled corn, bell peppers, jalapeño chile, vinegar, honey and salt in a bowl. Let stand for at least 1 hour before serving. Makes 1 1/2 cups.

Judge's Jailhouse Chili

4 pounds chili-ground beef
Bacon drippings (optional)
4 (4-ounce) cans tomato sauce
1 quart water
4 beef bouillon cubes
4 tablespoons dried garlic chips
1/2 cup chili powder, or to taste
3 tablespoons cumin
1/2 teaspoon cayenne pepper
Salt to taste
Chili beans (optional)
Chopped green onions (optional)

Brown the beef in bacon drippings in a skillet, stirring until crumbly; drain. Stir in the tomato sauce, water, bouillon cubes, garlic chips, chili powder, cumin, cayenne pepper and salt. Bring to a boil. Reduce the heat and simmer, covered, for 2 hours, stirring occasionally. Thicken slightly if desired with a mixture of flour and water. Add chili beans. Cook until heated through. Top each serving with a sprinkling of green onions. Makes 8 to 10 servings.

Note: *This is reported to be Liz Taylor's recipe for chili, which she calls "hot stuff."*

Fisherman's Pot

1 (15-ounce) can diced tomatoes
2 medium potatoes, finely chopped
1 cup chicken broth
1/2 cup each thinly sliced celery and onion
1 tablespoon sugar (optional)
1/2 teaspoon minced garlic
1 teaspoon parsley
1 teaspoon salt
Dash of thyme
1 pound mild white fish fillets, such as cod or orange roughy, cut into chunks
1/4 cup white wine

Combine the tomatoes, potatoes, broth, celery, onion, sugar, garlic, parsley, salt and thyme in a large saucepan. Cook, covered, over medium-high heat for 5 minutes. Reduce the heat to medium. Cook for 9 to 10 minutes longer, stirring once. Add the fish and wine. Cook, covered, for 10 minutes or until the fish flakes easily, stirring once. Makes 4 to 6 servings.

Cream of Pimento Soup

^{1}/4 cup (^{1}/2 stick) butter
^{1}/3 cup flour
2 (15-ounce) cans chicken broth
3 cups half-and-half
2 (4-ounce) jars diced pimentos, undrained
1 tablespoon grated onion
1 teaspoon salt
^{1}/2 teaspoon hot red pepper sauce
Chopped fresh chives

Melt the butter over low heat in a heavy saucepan. Whisk in the flour. Cook for 1 minute, stirring constantly. Add the broth and half-and-half gradually. Cook over medium heat until thick and bubbly, stirring constantly. Process the pimentos in a blender or food processor until smooth. Add the pimentos, onion, salt and hot sauce to the white sauce and stir well. Cook over low heat until heated through, stirring constantly. Chill, covered, for 8 hours. Heat the soup over medium heat for 8 to 10 minutes. Top each serving with a sprinkling of fresh chives. Makes 8 servings.

Note: *Try this soup served cold for a refreshing summer appetizer.*

There are two common methods of roasting peppers: over the gas stove and under the broiler. Regardless of the method that you choose, follow the same steps for great results. Cut a small slit in all peppers but bell peppers prior to roasting. As the skin blackens, watch closely so that the flesh does not burn. Once the pepper is blackened (it need not be completely black all over), immediately place in a sealable plastic bag and allow to steam until cool. Peel, seed, and slice or chop when cool.

When using a gas stove, arrange peppers on a wire rack above a medium flame. Turn frequently to blacken evenly on all sides. When using a broiler, place peppers on the rack of a broiler pan four to six inches under the heat source. Keep the oven door open.

Shrimp and Sausage Gumbo

²/3 cup flour
²/3 cup vegetable oil
1 pound smoked sausage,
cut into ¹/4-inch slices
2 cups chopped onions
²/3 cup chopped green bell pepper
¹/2 cup thinly sliced green onion tops
2 tablespoons minced fresh parsley
1 tablespoon minced garlic
¹/4 cup water
2 or 3 fish bouillon cubes
3 bay leaves
1 teaspoon thyme
Salt to taste
1¹/4 teaspoons freshly ground black pepper
¹/8 teaspoon cayenne pepper
2 quarts water
2 pounds shrimp, peeled, deveined
2¹/2 to 3 tablespoons filé powder
Cooked rice

Brown the flour slowly in the oil in a large soup pot until dark brown, stirring constantly. Add the sausage, onions, bell pepper, green onion tops, parsley and garlic. Cook over low heat for 10 minutes, stirring constantly. Add ¹/4 cup water, the bouillon cubes, bay leaves, thyme, salt, black pepper and cayenne pepper and stir well. Add 2 quarts water gradually. Bring to a boil, stirring gently. Reduce the heat and simmer for 45 minutes. Add the shrimp. Cook for 8 minutes longer. Remove from the heat. Add the filé powder and stir well. Let stand for 5 minutes. Serve the gumbo in deep bowls over rice. Makes 8 to 10 servings.

When buying garlic, look for heads that are firm with no green sprouts. Garlic should be kept at room temperature for no more than a month. The longer garlic sits, the stronger the flavor becomes. Garlic also becomes stronger the more it is minced or crushed. Burned garlic is bitter while roasted garlic has a sweet taste. To easily peel garlic, microwave the cloves on High for 15 to 30 seconds. Squeeze the end of each clove until the garlic pops out of its skin.

Shrimp Étouffée

3/4 cup (1 1/2 sticks) butter
4 cups chopped onions
2 cups chopped green bell peppers
2 cups chopped celery
2 teaspoons chopped garlic
2 pounds medium shrimp, peeled
2 teaspoons salt
1/2 teaspoon cayenne pepper
2 tablespoons flour
1 1/2 cups water
6 tablespoons chopped fresh parsley
1/2 cup sliced green onions
Hot cooked rice

Melt the butter over medium heat in a skillet. Add the onions, bell peppers and celery. Cook until the onions are tender. Add the garlic. Sauté for 1 to 2 minutes longer. Add the shrimp, salt and cayenne pepper. Cook for 3 to 5 minutes. Combine the flour and water and add to the shrimp mixture. Cook until the gumbo has thickened, stirring constantly. Reduce the heat and simmer for 3 to 5 minutes. Stir in the parsley and green onions. Serve over rice. Makes 6 to 8 servings.

Note: *This étouffée will keep for a day or two in the refrigerator.*

Gazpacho

2 cups diced peeled cucumber
2 cups diced red bell pepper
2 cups diced tomatoes
1/2 cup minced red onion
2 cups tomato juice or vegetable juice cocktail
1/2 cup red wine vinegar
1/3 cup extra-virgin olive oil
2 dashes of Tabasco sauce
Salt and pepper to taste
1 ripe avocado, diced

Combine the cucumber, bell pepper, tomatoes, onion, tomato juice, vinegar, olive oil, Tabasco sauce, salt and pepper in a large bowl. Process 1/2 of the vegetable mixture in a blender or food processor until smooth. Process the remaining 1/2. Combine the batches of purée in a large container and stir well. Chill for 8 hours. Top each serving with the avocado. Makes 6 to 8 servings.

Soups & Salads

Cream of Watercress Soup with Pan-Seared Scallops

6 medium leeks, chopped (white and
pale green parts only)
2 russet potatoes, peeled,
cut into 1-inch pieces
3 tablespoons butter
1 (49-ounce) can low-salt chicken broth
2 bunches watercress, trimmed,
coarsely chopped
2/3 cup sour cream
1 cup whole milk
Salt and pepper to taste
10 jumbo scallops
1 tablespoon vegetable oil
1 tablespoon butter
Sprigs of watercress

Sauté the leeks and potatoes in 3 tablespoons butter in a large saucepan for 4 minutes or until the leeks are tender. Add the broth. Bring to a boil. Reduce the heat and simmer, covered, for 20 minutes or until the potatoes are tender. Remove from the heat. Add 2 bunches watercress and let stand, covered, for 5 minutes or until the watercress wilts.

Purée the soup in batches in a blender. Return the purée to the saucepan and whisk in the sour cream. Thin with the milk to the desired consistency. Season with salt and pepper. Cook over low heat until heated through, stirring constantly.

Sauté the scallops in the oil and 1 tablespoon butter in a skillet over medium-high heat for 2 minutes on each side or until golden brown and just cooked through. Sprinkle with salt and pepper. Top each serving of soup with 1 scallop and garnish with watercress sprigs. Makes 10 servings.

Strawberry Soup

2 pints strawberries
4 cups water
1 1/2 cups sugar
1/2 teaspoon salt
1 cup sour cream
3/4 cup white wine
1 lime or lemon, sliced
1/2 cup sour cream
1 cup whipping cream, whipped
Sliced strawberries

Combine 2 pints strawberries and 2 cups of the water in a blender and process until smooth. Combine the purée, the remaining 2 cups water, sugar, salt, 1 cup sour cream, wine and lime slices in a saucepan. Cook over low heat, stirring constantly. Remove the lime slices. Fold 1/2 cup sour cream into the whipped cream. Top each serving of soup with a dollop of the whipped cream mixture and a few sliced strawberries. Serve the soup warm or chill the soup for 8 to 10 hours and serve cold. Makes 6 to 8 servings.

Zucchini Soup

1/2 cup chopped onion
1/2 cup diced green bell pepper
1 garlic clove, chopped
2 tablespoons butter
1 can chicken broth
1 cup chopped zucchini
1/2 cup shredded carrots
1/2 cup chopped fresh basil
Freshly ground pepper to taste
Chopped fresh parsley

Sauté the onion, bell pepper and garlic in the butter in a saucepan until the onion is tender. Stir in the broth, zucchini, carrots, basil and pepper. Bring to a boil. Reduce the heat and simmer for 10 minutes. Let stand until cool. Purée the soup in batches in a blender. Return the soup to a saucepan. Cook until heated through. Sprinkle each serving with freshly ground pepper and parsley. Makes 4 servings.

Broccoli Salad

1 cup mayonnaise
¹/4 cup milk
¹/4 cup sugar
1 tablespoon vinegar
1 large bunch broccoli, cut into small pieces
2 cups chopped celery
2 cups seedless red grapes
1 cup golden raisins
6 small green onions, chopped
8 ounces bacon, crisp-cooked, crumbled
1 cup chopped pecans or slivered almonds

Combine the mayonnaise, milk, sugar and vinegar in a small bowl and mix well. Chill until serving time.

To serve, combine the broccoli, celery, grapes, raisins and green onions in a salad bowl. Add the mayonnaise mixture, bacon and pecans and toss to combine. Makes 4 to 6 servings.

Lake Salad

1 cup light mayonnaise-type salad dressing
2 tablespoons (or more) sugar
1 to 2 tablespoons cider vinegar
2 or 3 broccoli crowns, separated into florets
¹/3 head cauliflower, separated into florets
3 or 4 carrots, chopped
¹/2 head cabbage, chopped
6 green onions, chopped
1 sweet onion, chopped
3 or 4 ribs celery, chopped
1 each green and red bell pepper, chopped
1 cup golden raisins
Sunflower seeds
Shredded cheese (optional)

Combine the salad dressing, sugar and vinegar in a small bowl and mix well. Chill for 4 hours or up to several days.

To serve, combine the broccoli florets, cauliflower florets, carrots, cabbage, green onions, onion, celery, bell peppers, raisins, sunflower seeds and cheese in a salad bowl. Add the salad dressing mixture and toss to combine. Makes 10 to 12 servings.

Chinese Chicken Salad

4 boneless skinless chicken breasts, cubed
$^1/_2$ cup sesame oil
$^1/_4$ cup soy sauce
$^1/_2$ teaspoon hot chile oil
3 garlic cloves, pressed
1 tablespoon grated fresh gingerroot, or
1 teaspoon dried ginger
Juice of 1 lemon
2 tablespoons peanut oil
2 tablespoons minced garlic
1 tablespoon grated fresh gingerroot
1 pound green beans, stemmed
Red pepper flakes to taste
$^1/_4$ cup soy sauce
1 tablespoon peanut oil
1 pound field greens
Oriental Dressing
Freshly ground black pepper to taste

Combine the chicken, sesame oil, $^1/_4$ cup soy sauce, hot chile oil, garlic, 1 tablespoon gingerroot and lemon juice in a sealable plastic bag. Marinate in the refrigerator for 4 to 24 hours.

Heat 2 tablespoons peanut oil in a wok over high heat for 2 minutes. Add the garlic and 1 tablespoon gingerroot. Stir-fry for 1 to 2 minutes. Add the green beans and red pepper flakes. Stir-fry for 5 minutes or until the green beans are tender-crisp. Stir in $^1/_4$ cup soy sauce and cook for 30 seconds. Remove the green beans to a bowl. Wipe the wok clean. Heat 1 tablespoon peanut oil in the wok and add the marinated chicken pieces. Stir-fry for 3 minutes or until cooked through. Toss the field greens with Oriental Dressing in a bowl. Arrange the greens on four plates. Top each with $^1/_4$ of the chicken pieces and the green beans. Sprinkle with pepper.
Makes 4 servings.

Oriental Dressing

2 tablespoons rice vinegar
Juice of $^1/_2$ lemon
1 tablespoon soy sauce
Freshly ground black pepper to taste
5 tablespoons extra-virgin olive oil
1 tablespoon sesame oil

Combine the vinegar, lemon juice, soy sauce and pepper in a small bowl. Add the olive oil and sesame oil in a steady stream, whisking constantly until blended. Makes about $^1/_2$ cup.

Chutney Chicken Salad

4 boneless skinless chicken breasts,
cooked, cubed
1 (16-ounce) package broccoli florets
4 green onions, chopped
1 medium red bell pepper, chopped
1 (6-ounce) package dried cranberries
Chutney Dressing
1/2 to 1 cup chopped peanuts (optional)

Combine the chicken, broccoli, green onions, bell pepper and dried cranberries in a salad bowl. Chill for 1 hour. Add Chutney Dressing and toss to combine. Sprinkle with the peanuts before serving. Makes 6 servings.

Note: *If you want a salad with a little less crunch, you can try this without the broccoli florets.*

Chutney Dressing

1 (9-ounce) jar chutney
1/2 cup mayonnaise
2 garlic cloves, minced
1/4 teaspoon crushed red pepper

Combine the chutney, mayonnaise, garlic and pepper in a small bowl and mix well. Makes 1 1/2 cups.

Chicken and Artichoke Salad

4 boneless skinless chicken breasts,
cooked, cubed
1 (14-ounce) can artichoke hearts,
drained, chopped
3/4 cup mayonnaise
3/4 cup chopped celery
5 green onions, chopped
1 cup toasted pecans, chopped
1/4 teaspoon salt
1/8 teaspoon each garlic powder and pepper

Combine the chicken, artichoke hearts, mayonnaise, celery, green onions, pecans, salt, garlic powder and pepper in a bowl and mix well. Chill until serving time. Makes 8 to 10 servings.

Note: *This salad is fine served on a bed of salad greens and sprinkled with parsley. For a fancier presentation, scoop the salad into avocado halves that have been rubbed with lemon juice.*

Chicken and Fruit Salad

2 cups chopped cooked chicken
1/2 cup chopped celery
8 ounces seedless grapes, halved
1/4 cup sliced water chestnuts
Curry Dressing or Cream Dressing
Boston or Bibb lettuce
1/2 cup toasted slivered almonds
8 ounces pineapple chunks, drained

Combine the chicken, celery, grapes and water chestnuts in a bowl. Add desired amount of Curry Dressing or Cream Dressing and toss to combine. Chill for 2 to 3 hours. Spoon the salad over the lettuce. Sprinkle with the almonds and garnish with the pineapple chunks. Makes 8 servings.

Note: *To dress up this salad a bit, try garnishing with fresh ripe pineapple slices rather than the canned pineapple chunks.*

Curry Dressing

3/4 cup mayonnaise
1 teaspoon curry powder
2 teaspoons soy sauce
2 teaspoons lemon juice

Combine the mayonnaise, curry powder, soy sauce and lemon juice in a small bowl and mix well. Makes 3/4 cup.

Cream Dressing

1 cup mayonnaise
1/2 cup stiffly whipped cream
2 tablespoons chopped fresh parsley
1/2 teaspoon salt

Mix the mayonnaise, whipped cream, parsley and salt in a small bowl. Makes 1 1/2 cups.

Soups & Salads

Chipotle Ranch Salad

Corn tortillas, cut into thin strips
Vegetable oil
Salt to taste
Assorted salad greens
Roma tomatoes, sliced
Feta cheese, crumbled
Chili Pecans
Chipotle Ranch Dressing

Let tortilla strips stand at room temperature for 15 minutes or until dry. Fry the tortilla strips in hot oil in a skillet; drain. Salt lightly. Combine desired amounts of the salad greens, tomatoes and cheese in a salad bowl. Add Chili Pecans and Chipotle Ranch Dressing and toss. Top with tortilla crisps. Makes variable servings.

Chili Pecans

2 cups pecans or walnuts
1/4 cup melted butter
2 tablespoons chili powder
1 tablespoon sugar
1 teaspoon each salt and cayenne pepper
2 tablespoons minced fresh parsley

Toast the pecans at 300 degrees for 8 minutes. Combine the toasted pecans, butter, chili powder, sugar, salt, cayenne pepper and parsley in a bowl and mix well. Bake the pecans in a single layer on a baking sheet at 325 degrees for 10 to 15 minutes. Cool on paper towels. Store the pecans in a covered container.

Chipotle Ranch Dressing

2 to 3 cups Ranch-style dressing
1 canned chipotle chile with adobo sauce, chopped
1 tablespoon minced fresh parsley or cilantro
1 to 2 tablespoons chili sauce
1 to 2 teaspoons lime juice
Pinch of salt

Combine the dressing, chipotle chile, parsley, chili sauce, lime juice and salt in a bowl and mix well. Makes 2 to 3 cups.

Sugared Almond
Strawberry Salad

1 head Bibb lettuce, torn
1 head leaf lettuce, torn
1 can mandarin oranges, drained
10 fresh strawberries, thinly sliced
2 green onions, chopped
Sugared Almonds
Poppy Seed Dressing or Orange Dressing

Combine the Bibb lettuce, leaf lettuce, oranges, strawberries, green onions and Sugared Almonds in a salad bowl. Add the desired amount of Poppy Seed Dressing or Orange Dressing and toss to combine. Makes 6 servings.

Note: *This recipe becomes a delicious spinach salad if you substitute baby spinach leaves for the lettuce. It's equally good with either dressing.*

Sugared Almonds

1 egg white, at room temperature
$^1/4$ cup sugar
1 cup sliced almonds
1 tablespoon melted butter

Beat the egg white in a mixing bowl until soft peaks form. Add the sugar gradually, beating until stiff peaks form. Fold in the almonds. Coat a baking dish with the melted butter. Spread the almonds over the butter. Bake at 325 degrees for 20 to 25 minutes or until the almonds are dry, stirring every 5 minutes. Cool completely. Freeze in sealable plastic freezer bags for future use if desired. Makes 1 cup.

Poppy Seed Dressing

²/3 cup vegetable oil
¹/2 cup sugar
¹/4 cup balsamic vinegar
1 tablespoon plus 1 teaspoon poppy seeds
1 teaspoon prepared mustard
¹/2 teaspoon salt

Combine the oil, sugar, vinegar, poppy seeds, mustard and salt in a jar and shake well. Makes 1¹/2 cups.

Orange Dressing

³/4 cup olive oil
¹/4 cup blood orange vinegar
2 tablespoons orange juice
1 teaspoon grated orange zest
¹/2 teaspoon poppy seeds
¹/8 teaspoon salt
¹/8 teaspoon pepper

Whisk the olive oil, vinegar, orange juice, orange zest, poppy seeds, salt and pepper together in a small bowl until well blended. Makes 1 cup.

Oriental Salad

2 heads romaine, torn
4 green onions, chopped
10 to 12 strawberries, thinly sliced
1 (11-ounce) can mandarin oranges, drained
1 cup pecans or walnuts
3 ounces ramen noodles, broken in pieces
(discard the flavor pack)
1/4 cup (1/2 stick) butter
1 cup olive oil
1/2 cup balsamic vinegar
1/2 cup sugar
4 teaspoons soy sauce
1 tablespoon teriyaki sauce
Pinch of ginger
Pepper to taste

Combine the romaine, green onions, strawberries and oranges in a bowl. Cook the pecans and ramen noodles in the butter in a skillet until brown. Combine the olive oil, vinegar, sugar, soy sauce, teriyaki sauce, ginger and pepper in a jar and shake well. Add the pecan mixture and desired amount of the dressing to the salad and toss to combine. Makes 8 to 10 servings.

Fancy Mixed Greens

Mixed salad greens
1 (3-ounce) package slivered almonds, toasted
1 bunch green onions, chopped
2 (3-ounce) packages Parmesan cheese
1 cup vegetable oil
1/2 cup vinegar
1/2 cup sugar
1 teaspoon celery seeds
1 teaspoon each onion juice and garlic juice

Combine the greens, almonds, green onions and cheese in a salad bowl. Combine the oil, vinegar, sugar, celery seeds, onion juice and garlic juice in a jar and shake well. Pour over the greens and toss to combine. Makes 6 servings.

Autumn Tossed Salad

1/2 cup sugar
1/3 cup red wine vinegar
2 tablespoons lemon juice
2 tablespoons chopped onion
1/2 teaspoon salt
2/3 cup safflower oil
2 to 3 teaspoons poppy seeds
10 cups torn romaine
1 cup (4 ounces) shredded Swiss cheese
1/4 cup dried cranberries
1 medium apple, cored, cubed (not peeled)
1 medium pear, cored, cubed (not peeled)
1/2 to 1 cup chopped cashews

Combine the sugar, vinegar, lemon juice, onion and salt in a blender or food processor and process until smooth. Add the safflower oil gradually while the blender is running. Add the poppy seeds and process briefly. Chill until serving time. Combine the romaine, cheese, dried cranberries, apple and pear in a salad bowl. Add the desired amount of poppy seed mixture and the cashews. Toss to combine. Makes 8 to 10 servings.

Wild Rice and Chicken Salad

1 cup wild rice
1 can chicken broth
1 cup (or more) diced cooked chicken
1 1/2 cups green grapes, halved
1 cup cashews
1 cup coarsely chopped cooked artichoke bottoms or water chestnuts
Chopped red or green onions (optional)
1 cup mayonnaise
1 1/2 teaspoons seasoned salt

Combine the wild rice and broth in a casserole dish and place the dish in an unheated oven. Heat the oven to 500 degrees. Turn off the oven and let the dish stand in the oven for 8 to 10 hours. Chill the rice until serving time. Combine the rice, chicken, grapes, cashews, artichokes and onions in a salad bowl and mix well. Stir in the mayonnaise and seasoned salt. Serve the salad chilled or at room temperature on lettuce leaves. Makes 6 to 8 servings.

Artichoke and Rice Salad

4 cups chicken stock
2 cups rice
3 (6-ounce) jars marinated artichokes,
drained, marinade reserved
5 green onions, chopped
1 (4-ounce) jar pimento-stuffed
olives, chopped
1 large green bell pepper, diced
3 large ribs celery, diced
1/4 cup chopped fresh parsley
2 cups mayonnaise
1 teaspoon curry powder
Salt and pepper to taste

Bring the stock to a boil in a saucepan and stir
in the rice. Return to a boil. Reduce the heat and
simmer for 20 minutes or until the liquid is
absorbed. Let cool. Chop the artichokes and add
with the green onions, olives, bell pepper, celery
and parsley to the rice. Combine the mayonnaise,
reserved artichoke marinade, curry powder, salt and
pepper in a bowl and mix well. Add to the rice
and mix well. Makes 8 servings.

Pork and Wild Rice Salad

2 pork tenderloins in teriyaki marinade
6 cups cooked wild rice
2 cups sugar snap peas
2 (11-ounce) cans mandarin oranges, drained
2 cans sliced water chestnuts
1/3 cup olive oil
1/3 cup rice vinegar
5 tablespoons soy sauce
1/4 cup toasted sesame seeds
2 teaspoons ginger

Roast or grill the pork using the package directions.
Cut into thin slices. Combine the pork, rice, peas,
oranges and water chestnuts in a salad bowl. Mix the
olive oil, vinegar, soy sauce, sesame seeds and ginger
in a jar. Pour over the salad mixture and toss gently.
Serve the salad at room temperature or chilled.
Makes 15 to 18 servings.

Wild Rice Shrimp Salad

1 pound frozen peeled cooked shrimp, thawed
1 (6-ounce) package wild rice mix
1 (7-ounce) jar marinated artichoke quarters,
drained, marinade reserved
4 green onions, chopped
1/2 cup chopped green bell pepper
12 black olives, sliced
1 rib celery, chopped
1 can mandarin oranges, drained (optional)
1/3 cup mayonnaise
3/4 teaspoon curry powder

Chop the shrimp, reserving a few whole for the garnish. Prepare the rice using the package directions. Combine the shrimp, rice, artichokes, green onions, bell pepper, olives, celery and oranges in a salad bowl. Combine 3 tablespoons reserved artichoke marinade, the mayonnaise and curry powder in a bowl and mix well. Add to the rice mixture. Garnish with the reserved whole shrimp. Chill, covered, for 5 hours. Serve over lettuce. Makes 6 to 8 servings.

Basic Shrimp Boil

1 gallon water (no salt added)
1 (3-ounce) bag crab boil
1 lemon, halved
6 to 10 bay leaves
3 tablespoons white distilled vinegar
1 tablespoon unsalted butter
1 1/2 pounds fresh medium shrimp, unpeeled
4 to 5 tablespoons Old Bay
seasoning (optional)

Combine the water, crab boil, lemon halves, bay leaves, vinegar and butter in a large Dutch oven or soup pot. Bring to a boil. Stir the crab boil bag around to release the flavors. Boil, loosely covered, for 1 to 2 minutes. Add 1/2 to 3/4 pound of the shrimp. Return to a boil. Cook until the shrimp float to the top and turn pink. Remove the shrimp. Repeat with additional batches of shrimp, adding them gradually to the same broth. Sprinkle the shrimp generously with the Old Bay seasoning. Peel and eat. Makes 4 servings.

Chapter Recipes

Brunch & Breads

Brunch Miniature Pizzas

2 pounds bulk pork sausage
1 cup (2 sticks) margarine, softened
4 jars Old English processed cheese spread
24 English muffins, split

Brown the sausage in a skillet, stirring until crumbly; drain. Combine the margarine and cheese spread in a bowl and mix well. Stir in the sausage. Spoon the sausage mixture on the muffin halves, spreading to the edges. Bake on a baking sheet at 350 degrees for 10 to 15 minutes. Serve immediately. Makes 48 servings.

Note: *To prepare the pizzas ahead of time, simply freeze them on the baking sheet and store the frozen pizzas in sealable plastic freezer bags.*

Eggs Lorraine

2 tablespoons butter
1 cup (4 ounces) shredded Swiss cheese
1 cup (4 ounces) shredded Cheddar cheese
8 eggs
1/2 cup heavy cream
Salt and pepper to taste
8 slices bacon, crisp-cooked, crumbled

Spread the butter in an 8×10-inch baking dish. Sprinkle 1/2 of the Swiss cheese and 1/2 of the Cheddar cheese over the butter. Beat the eggs with the cream, salt and pepper in a bowl; pour over the cheese layer. Top with the remaining Swiss cheese, Cheddar cheese and bacon. Bake at 350 degrees for 20 to 25 minutes. Makes 6 to 8 servings.

Note: *This easy-to-assemble dish is great right out of the oven, but it also reheats well in the microwave.*

May Fair Casserole

1 pound hot bulk pork sausage
1 pound mild bulk pork sausage
2 boxes onion and garlic croutons
4 eggs
2^{1}/2 cups milk
^{1}/2 teaspoon dry mustard
1 (4-ounce) can diced green chiles, drained
1 (2-ounce) jar diced pimento, drained
2 cups (8 ounces) shredded sharp
Cheddar cheese
2 cups (8 ounces) shredded Velveeta cheese
1 (10-ounce) can cream of mushroom soup
^{1}/2 cup milk

Brown the sausage in a skillet, stirring until crumbly; drain. Spread the sausage in a 9×13-inch baking dish. Layer the croutons over the sausage. Beat the eggs, 2^{1}/2 cups milk and the dry mustard together in a bowl. Stir in the green chiles and pimento. Pour the egg mixture over the croutons. Sprinkle with the Cheddar cheese and Velveeta cheese. Chill, covered, for 8 to 10 hours. Combine the soup and ^{1}/2 cup milk in a bowl and mix well. Pour over the cheese. Bake at 350 degrees for 45 minutes. Makes 10 servings.

Ham Soufflé

16 slices bread, crusts removed
2 cups (8 ounces) shredded sharp
Cheddar cheese
2 cups chopped cooked ham
6 eggs
3 cups milk
^{1}/2 teaspoon salt
1 tablespoon dry mustard
2 cups crushed cornflakes
^{1}/2 cup (1 stick) butter, melted

Arrange ^{1}/2 of the bread slices in a buttered 9×13-inch baking dish. Layer the cheese and ham over the bread. Top with the remaining bread slices. Beat the eggs, milk, salt and dry mustard together in a bowl and pour over the bread. Chill, covered, for 8 to 10 hours. Let the casserole come to room temperature before baking. Combine the cornflakes and butter in a bowl and sprinkle over the casserole. Bake at 350 degrees for 1 hour. Makes 8 servings.

Note: *For a smaller breakfast or brunch crowd, halve the recipe and bake in an 8×8-inch pan.*

Chile Egg Puff

10 eggs
1/2 cup flour
1 teaspoon baking powder
1 teaspoon salt
16 ounces creamed small curd cottage cheese
4 cups (1 pound) shredded
Monterey Jack cheese
1/2 cup (1 stick) butter, melted
2 (4-ounce) cans diced green chiles

Beat the eggs in a mixing bowl until thick and pale yellow. Add the flour, baking powder, salt, cottage cheese, Monterey Jack cheese and butter and beat until smooth. Stir in the green chiles. Pour into a buttered 9×13-inch dish. Bake at 350 degrees for 30 minutes or until firm in the center. Makes 10 to 12 servings.

Note: *This dish works well as an appetizer as well as a brunch dish; cut the puff into smaller servings. For a spicier dish, just increase the amount of green chiles.*

Miniature Omelets

1 red bell pepper
1 green bell pepper
1 onion, diced
1 teaspoon each olive oil and butter
12 eggs
2 cups sour cream
2 cups (8 ounces) shredded
Monterey Jack cheese
2 cups (8 ounces) shredded Cheddar cheese
8 ounces ham, finely chopped

Broil the bell peppers until blackened, turning frequently. Enclose the hot peppers in a sealable plastic bag for 10 to 15 minutes. Peel, seed and dice the peppers. Sauté the onion in the olive oil and butter in a skillet until light brown. Process the eggs and sour cream in a blender until smooth. Mix the egg mixture, bell peppers, onion, cheeses and ham in a bowl. Pour into muffin cups coated with nonstick cooking spray. Bake at 375 degrees for 15 to 20 minutes or until light brown. Makes 12 servings.

Note: *For bite-size servings, bake the omelets in miniature muffin cups. Adjust the cooking time accordingly.*

Zesty Sausage Balls

2 pounds ground bulk pork sausage
2 cups (8 ounces) shredded Cheddar cheese
2 cups baking mix
10 ounces apricot jelly
1/2 cup barbecue sauce

Combine the sausage, cheese and baking mix in a bowl and mix well. Roll into small balls. Bake at 350 degrees for 15 to 20 minutes; drain well. Combine the sausage balls, apricot jelly and barbecue sauce in a saucepan. Cook over low heat for 20 minutes. Remove to a chafing dish and serve warm with wooden picks. Makes about 100 servings.

Note: *The sweet and tangy sauce is what makes the difference in these sausage balls. These are great as an appetizer as well as a brunch dish.*

Sausage Spirals

1 pound bulk pork sausage
4 ounces cream cheese with chives
1 (10-count) can crescent rolls
1 egg white, beaten
2 teaspoons poppy seeds

Brown the sausage in a skillet, stirring until crumbly; drain. Add the cream cheese and stir well. Unroll the crescent roll dough and separate into 2 rectangles. Shape the sausage mixture into 2 logs and place 1 log on each rectangle. Roll as for a jelly roll, sealing the edges. Place seam side down on a nonstick baking sheet. Brush with the egg white and sprinkle with the poppy seeds. Bake for 20 minutes or until golden brown. Cut into 1-inch slices. Serve hot. Makes 20 servings.

Swedish Coffee Cake

1 cup (2 sticks) butter or margarine, softened
2 cups sugar
2 eggs
1 cup sour cream
1/2 teaspoon vanilla extract
2 cups cake flour, sifted
1 1/4 teaspoons baking powder
1/4 teaspoon salt
1 cup chopped pecans
1 tablespoon firmly packed brown sugar
1 teaspoon cinnamon
Confectioners' sugar to taste

Cream the butter, sugar and eggs in a bowl until light and fluffy. Fold in the sour cream and vanilla. Sift the flour, baking powder and salt together. Add to the sour cream mixture and mix well. Spoon 1/2 of the batter into a greased and floured tube pan. Combine the pecans, brown sugar and cinnamon and sprinkle 1/2 of the mixture over the batter. Layer the remaining batter and pecan mixture over the top. Bake at 350 degrees for 1 hour. Sprinkle the cake with confectioners' sugar while still warm. Cool in the pan. Invert onto a serving plate. Makes 16 servings.

Fluffy Pancakes

1 cup flour
2 teaspoons baking powder
1 teaspoon baking soda
1 teaspoon salt
2 eggs, beaten
2 cups buttermilk

Combine the flour, baking powder, baking soda and salt in a bowl and mix well. Beat the eggs with the buttermilk in a bowl. Add to the dry ingredients and stir just until mixed. Pour 1/4 cup at a time onto a hot lightly greased griddle. Cook until brown on both sides, turning once. Serve with butter and hot syrup. Makes 12 (4-inch) pancakes.

Stuffed French Toast with Grand Marnier Fruit Sauce

12 (1¹/2-inch-thick) slices French bread
1 (8-ounce) package cream cheese, softened
2 tablespoons sugar
¹/2 teaspoon nutmeg
¹/2 teaspoon cinnamon
6 eggs
1 cup half-and-half
¹/2 cup milk
Grand Marnier Fruit Sauce

Cut a horizontal pocket in each bread slice. Combine the cream cheese, sugar, nutmeg and cinnamon in a bowl and mix well. Spoon about 1¹/2 teaspoons of the cream cheese mixture into each bread pocket, spreading evenly. Place 8 of the bread slices in a buttered 8×12-inch baking dish and the remaining 4 slices in a buttered 8×8-inch baking dish. Beat the eggs with the half-and-half and milk in a bowl. Pour evenly over the bread slices, turning the slices to coat evenly. Bake at 350 degrees for 35 minutes or until golden brown. Serve immediately with Grand Marnier Fruit Sauce. Makes 12 servings.

Note: *To make this dish ahead of time, prepare as directed, but do not bake. Chill, covered, for up to 24 hours. Let stand for 30 minutes before baking.*

Grand Marnier Fruit Sauce

1 cup sifted confectioners' sugar
2 tablespoons cornstarch
¹/2 cup (1 stick) unsalted butter, melted
¹/3 cup Grand Marnier
3 cups sliced fresh strawberries

Combine the confectioners' sugar and cornstarch in a saucepan and mix well. Add the butter and stir until mixed. Stir in the Grand Marnier. Bring to a boil over medium heat, stirring constantly. Boil for 1 minute, stirring constantly. Add the strawberries. Cook for 1 minute longer. Makes 3 cups.

Crème Brûlée French Toast

1/2 cup (1 stick) unsalted butter
1 cup firmly packed brown sugar
2 tablespoons corn syrup
6 (1-inch-thick) slices from center of round
country-style bread, crusts trimmed
5 eggs
1 1/2 cups half-and-half
1 teaspoon vanilla extract
1 teaspoon Grand Marnier
1/4 teaspoon salt

Combine the butter, brown sugar and corn syrup in a small saucepan over medium heat. Cook until smooth, stirring constantly. Pour into a 9×13-inch baking dish. Arrange the bread slices over the butter mixture. Beat the eggs with the half-and-half, vanilla, Grand Marnier and salt in a bowl. Pour evenly over the bread. Chill, covered, for 8 to 24 hours. Let stand at room temperature before baking. Bake, uncovered, at 350 degrees for 35 to 40 minutes or until puffed and the edges are golden. Makes 6 servings.

The Montford Inn

The photo on the opening page of this chapter was taken at the Montford Inn. Nestled in the heart of Norman, Oklahoma, Montford Inn Bed and Breakfast invites you to experience the comfort of being at home, yet being a part of something special. The inn offers everything the discriminating guest has come to expect from a good B&B: elegant rooms furnished with antiques, a delightfully romantic and relaxing atmosphere, great comfort, and an attention to detail. Built in 1994, the inn was custom-designed to incorporate both elegance and country tradition.

Pecan Waffles with Caramelized Bananas

1 cup flour
1/2 cup pecans, toasted, finely chopped
1 teaspoon baking powder
1/4 teaspoon baking soda
1/2 teaspoon salt
1 egg, lightly beaten
1 cup buttermilk
6 tablespoons unsalted butter, melted
Caramelized Bananas

Combine the flour, pecans, baking powder, baking soda and salt in a bowl. Beat the egg with the buttermilk and butter in a bowl. Add to the dry ingredients and stir just until mixed. Pour 1/2 of the batter onto a hot lightly greased waffle iron. Spread the batter evenly to make four 4-inch waffles. Cook using the manufacturer's instructions. Remove the waffles to a baking sheet in a 250-degree oven. Repeat the process with the remaining batter. Place 1 waffle on each of 4 serving plates. Spoon 1/4 of the Caramelized Bananas over each waffle. Top each with a second waffle. Makes 4 servings.

Caramelized Bananas

3 large firm ripe bananas
3/4 cup sugar
2 tablespoons unsalted butter, melted

Cut each banana in half crosswise and then lengthwise. Roll the bananas in the sugar to coat. Heat the butter in a large nonstick skillet over medium-high heat until the foam subsides. Add the bananas cut side down. Cook until golden brown, turning once. Remove to a greased baking sheet and let cool slightly. Makes 4 servings.

Orange Currant Scones

2 cups flour
2 tablespoons sugar
1 tablespoon baking powder
1/2 teaspoon salt
1/2 cup (1 stick) unsalted butter, chilled,
cut into small pieces
1/2 cup currants
1 egg
1/2 cup heavy cream
Zest of 1 orange

Combine the flour, sugar, baking powder and salt in a food processor. Add the butter and process until crumbly. Remove to a bowl. Stir in the currants. Beat the egg with the cream and orange zest in a bowl. Add to the flour mixture and stir to form large clumps of dough. Knead gently on a floured surface to form a soft dough. Roll into a 10-inch circle 3/4 inch thick. Cut into 8 wedges and press each wedge into a well of a lightly greased scone pan. Bake at 350 degrees for 25 minutes or until golden. Invert over a wire rack to remove the scones. Let cool for 10 minutes. Serve warm. Makes 8 servings.

Cream Biscuits

4 cups flour
2 tablespoons sugar
2 tablespoons baking powder
2 teaspoons salt
2 1/2 cups (or more) whipping cream
2/3 cup butter, melted

Combine the flour, sugar, baking powder and salt in a large bowl. Stir in enough cream to make a soft dough. Knead the dough on a lightly floured surface for 2 minutes or until smooth. Pat into a 1/2-inch-thick round. Cut into 2 1/2-inch rounds and dip in the butter, coating the top and sides. Arrange the biscuits butter side up on a nonstick baking sheet. Knead scraps of dough together and cut remaining biscuits. Chill, covered, until serving time. Bake at 425 degrees for 12 minutes or until light brown. Let cool slightly. Makes 24 servings.

Cream Cheese Breakfast Pastry

1 envelope dry yeast
$1/4$ cup warm (100- to 120-degree) water
1 teaspoon sugar
1 egg, lightly beaten
2 cups flour, sifted
$1/4$ teaspoon salt
$3/4$ cup ($1^1/2$ sticks) butter
2 (8-ounce) packages cream cheese
1 cup sugar
1 teaspoon lemon juice
Confectioners' sugar to taste

Combine the yeast with the water and 1 teaspoon sugar in a small bowl. Let stand for 10 minutes. Stir in the egg. Combine the flour and salt in a bowl. Cut in the butter until crumbly. Add the yeast mixture and stir just until mixed. Divide the dough into 2 balls and roll each into an 8×10-inch rectangle on a lightly floured surface.

Combine the cream cheese, 1 cup sugar and lemon juice in a bowl and mix well. Spread each rectangle with $1/2$ of the cream cheese mixture, leaving a 1-inch edge. Roll as for a jelly roll, sealing the edge and ends. Place seam side down on a greased baking sheet. Bake at 375 degrees for 25 minutes. Cool on a wire rack. Sprinkle with confectioners' sugar and slice into serving-size pieces. Makes 10 to 15 servings.

Old-Fashioned Honey Wheat Bread

1 1/2 cups water
1 cup creamed cottage cheese
1/2 cup honey
1/4 cup (1/2 stick) butter
5 1/2 cups all-purpose or unbleached flour
1 cup whole wheat flour
2 tablespoons sugar
1 tablespoon salt
2 envelopes dry yeast
1 egg
Melted butter (optional)

Heat the water, cottage cheese, honey and butter in a saucepan until very warm (120 to 130 degrees). Combine with 2 cups of the all-purpose flour, the whole wheat flour, sugar, salt, yeast and egg in a mixing bowl. Beat at low speed just until mixed. Beat at medium speed for 2 minutes. Stir in enough remaining all-purpose flour to make a stiff dough. Knead on a floured surface for 2 minutes or until smooth and elastic. Place in a greased bowl, turning to coat the surface. Let rise, covered, in a warm place for 45 to 60 minutes or until doubled in bulk.

Punch the dough down. Shape into 2 loaves. Place in 2 greased 5×9-inch or 4×8-inch loaf pans. Let rise, covered, in a warm place until doubled in bulk. Bake at 350 degrees for 40 to 50 minutes or until the loaves are deep golden brown and sound hollow when tapped. Remove from the pans. Cool on a wire rack. Brush the warm loaves with melted butter. Makes 2 loaves.

Caraway Cheese Bread

1 1/2 cups water
1 (11-ounce) can Cheddar cheese soup
2 tablespoons margarine
7 1/2 cups flour
2 envelopes dry yeast
2 tablespoons sugar
1 tablespoon salt
1 tablespoon caraway seeds
1/4 cup (1 ounce) grated Parmesan cheese
2 eggs

Combine the water, soup and margarine in a saucepan and heat until lukewarm. Combine 3 cups of the flour, the yeast, sugar, salt, caraway seeds and cheese in a mixing bowl. Add the soup mixture and eggs. Beat at low speed just until mixed. Beat at medium speed for 3 minutes. Stir in enough of the remaining flour to make a stiff dough. Knead on a floured surface for 5 minutes or until smooth and elastic. Place in a greased bowl, turning to coat the surface. Let rise, covered, in a warm place until doubled in bulk. Punch the dough down and divide into halves. Roll each half into a 7×14-inch rectangle. Roll as for a jelly roll, pressing the ends of the dough into the roll at each turn. Place in 2 greased 5×9-inch loaf pans. Let rise, covered, in a warm place until doubled in bulk. Bake at 375 degrees for 35 to 40 minutes or until golden brown. Remove from the pans. Cool on a wire rack. Makes 2 loaves.

Raisin and Caraway Irish Soda Bread

5 cups flour
1 cup sugar
1 tablespoon baking powder
1 1/2 teaspoons salt
1 teaspoon baking soda
1/2 cup (1 stick) unsalted butter,
cubed, softened
2 1/2 cups raisins
3 tablespoons caraway seeds
2 1/2 cups buttermilk
1 egg

Mix the flour, sugar, baking powder, salt and baking soda in a bowl. Cut in the butter until crumbly. Stir in the raisins and caraway seeds. Beat the buttermilk and egg together in a bowl. Stir into the dry ingredients to make a sticky dough. Spoon the dough into a buttered heavy ovenproof 10- to 12-inch skillet. Mound the dough slightly in the center and smooth the surface. Cut a 1-inch-deep "x" in the top center of the dough using a sharp knife dipped in flour. Bake at 350 degrees for 1 1/4 hours or until the loaf tests done. Cool in the skillet for 10 minutes. Remove to a wire rack to cool completely. Makes 1 loaf.

Spiced Apricot Bread

1 1/2 cups dried apricots, chopped
1 cup water
1 cup sugar
6 tablespoons shortening
1/2 teaspoon cinnamon
1/2 teaspoon ground cloves
1/4 teaspoon nutmeg
1/2 teaspoon salt
1 egg, beaten
2 cups flour
1 teaspoon baking soda

Combine the apricots, water, sugar, shortening, cinnamon, cloves, nutmeg and salt in a saucepan. Bring to a boil over medium heat. Reduce the heat and simmer for 5 minutes. Cool to lukewarm. Beat in the egg. Sift the flour and baking soda in a bowl. Add to the apricot mixture and stir just until mixed. Pour into a greased loaf pan. Bake at 350 degrees for 40 to 45 minutes or until the loaf tests done. Cool in the pan for 10 minutes. Remove to a wire rack to cool completely. Makes 1 loaf.

Cheddar and Chive Beer Bread

3 cups self-rising flour
1/2 cup sugar
1 (12-ounce) bottle beer
3/4 cup (3 ounces) shredded Cheddar cheese
2 tablespoons chopped fresh chives
1/4 cup (1/2 stick) butter or margarine, melted

Combine the flour, sugar, beer, cheese and chives in a bowl and mix well. Pour into a lightly greased 5×9-inch loaf pan. Bake at 350 degrees for 45 minutes. Pour the butter over the top. Bake for 10 minutes longer. Makes 1 loaf.

Cranberry Nut Bread

2 cups all-purpose or unbleached flour
1 cup sugar
1 1/2 teaspoons baking powder
1/2 teaspoon baking soda
1 teaspoon salt
1/4 cup shortening or margarine
1 teaspoon grated orange zest
3/4 cup orange juice
1 egg, lightly beaten
1 cup fresh or frozen cranberries, coarsely chopped
1/2 cup chopped nuts

Combine the flour, sugar, baking powder, baking soda and salt in a mixing bowl. Cut in the shortening until crumbly. Stir in the orange zest, orange juice and egg just until mixed. Fold in the cranberries and nuts. Pour into a greased 5×9-inch loaf pan. Bake at 350 degrees for 50 to 60 minutes or until the loaf tests done. Cool for 10 minutes. Remove to a wire rack to cool completely. Makes 1 loaf.

The best method for preparing quick breads is to combine the wet and dry ingredients separately first, then mix just until moistened. Too much mixing will make the dough tough and may cause air pockets to form.

Dutch Coffee Bread

 $^1/_2$ cup (1 stick) butter or margarine, softened
2 cups sugar
2 eggs
4 cups flour
2 teaspoons baking soda
1 teaspoon salt
2 cups buttermilk
 $^1/_2$ cup sugar
1 teaspoon cinnamon
Dots of butter or margarine

Cream the butter and 2 cups sugar in a mixing bowl until light and fluffy. Beat in the eggs. Mix the flour, baking soda and salt together. Add to the egg mixture alternately with the buttermilk, mixing well after each addition. Combine $^1/_2$ cup sugar and the cinnamon in a small bowl. Layer the batter and cinnamon sugar $^1/_3$ at a time in a greased and floured 4×8-inch loaf pan, ending with the cinnamon sugar. Dot with butter. Bake at 350 degrees for 1 hour or until the loaf tests done. Cool in the pan for 10 minutes. Remove to a wire rack to cool completely. Makes 1 loaf.

Note: *This recipe would be attractive baked in a bundt pan.*

Zucchini Date Bread with Pineapple Spread

3 cups flour
1 teaspoon baking soda
3/4 teaspoon salt
1 1/2 teaspoons cinnamon
1/8 teaspoon nutmeg
1 1/2 cups chopped pecans
3/4 cup chopped dates
1 cup sugar
3/4 cup firmly packed brown sugar
1 cup vegetable oil
1/4 cup plus 2 tablespoons milk
2 teaspoons vanilla extract
2 cups shredded peeled zucchini
Pineapple Spread

Combine the flour, baking soda, salt, cinnamon and nutmeg in a mixing bowl. Stir in the pecans and dates. Add the sugar, brown sugar, oil, milk, and vanilla and stir just until mixed. Fold in the zucchini. Pour the batter into 12 greased and sugared miniature bundt pans or individual loaf pans, filling 2/3 full. Bake at 325 degrees for 30 to 35 minutes. Cool on a wire rack. Wrap tightly to store. Serve the bread with Pineapple Spread. Makes 12 miniature loaves.

Pineapple Spread

1 (8-ounce) package cream cheese, softened
3 tablespoons confectioners' sugar
1 tablespoon pineapple juice
1/2 teaspoon vanilla extract
3 tablespoons drained crushed pineapple
2 tablespoons chopped pecans

Combine the cream cheese, confectioners' sugar, pineapple juice, vanilla, pineapple and pecans in a mixing bowl. Beat at medium speed for 1 minute. Chill, covered, until serving time. Makes 1 1/2 cups.

Pumpkin Bread

3¹/2 cups flour, sifted
2 teaspoons each baking soda and cinnamon
1 teaspoon salt
3 cups sugar
2 cups pumpkin
1 cup vegetable oil
²/3 cup water
4 eggs, lightly beaten
4 teaspoons vanilla extract
1 cup pecans, chopped
1 cup shredded coconut
1 cup raisins

Combine the flour, baking soda, cinnamon and salt in a bowl and mix well. Combine the sugar, pumpkin, oil, water, eggs and vanilla in a bowl and beat until well combined. Add to the dry ingredients and stir just until mixed. Stir in the pecans, coconut and raisins. Spoon the batter into 3 greased and floured loaf pans. Bake at 350 degrees for 1 hour or until the loaves test done. Cool on a wire rack. Makes 3 loaves.

Butterscotch Pumpkin Muffins

1³/4 cups flour
¹/2 cup packed light brown sugar
¹/2 cup sugar
1 teaspoon each baking soda and cinnamon
¹/4 teaspoon each baking powder and salt
¹/2 teaspoon each ginger and mace
¹/8 teaspoon ground cloves
2 eggs
1 cup pumpkin
¹/2 cup (1 stick) butter, melted
³/4 to 1 cup butterscotch chips
¹/2 cup chopped pecans, toasted (optional)

Mix the first 10 ingredients in a bowl. Beat the eggs with the pumpkin and butter in a bowl. Stir in the butterscotch chips and pecans. Stir into the dry ingredients just until mixed. Spoon the batter evenly into 18 greased muffin cups. Bake at 350 degrees for 20 to 25 minutes or until the muffins test done. Cool on a wire rack. Makes 18 muffins.

Note: *Toasting the pecans makes a big difference in the taste. The extra few minutes of time needed to toast the nuts is well worth the effort.*

Cranberry Butter

3/4 cup cranberries
6 tablespoons confectioners' sugar
2 teaspoons grated lemon zest
1 cup (2 sticks) unsalted butter,
cut into pieces, softened

Combine the cranberries, confectioners' sugar and lemon zest in a food processor and pulse until the cranberries are coarsely chopped. Add the butter and pulse just until mixed. Chill, covered, until serving time. Bring to room temperature before serving. Makes $1^1/2$ cups.

Orange Grand Marnier Butter

$^1/4$ cup ($^1/2$ stick) unsalted butter, softened
$^1/4$ cup cream cheese, softened
2 tablespoons orange zest
2 tablespoons Grand Marnier

Combine the butter, cream cheese, orange zest and Grand Marnier in a blender or food processor and process until smooth. Spoon into a mold. Chill until serving time. Unmold the butter and serve at room temperature. Makes $^1/2$ cup.

Royal Rosemary Butter

$^1/2$ cup (1 stick) unsalted butter, softened
1 tablespoon fresh rosemary leaves
2 or 3 garlic cloves
$^1/2$ teaspoon grated lemon zest
1 tablespoon lemon juice
$^1/4$ teaspoon red pepper flakes
Salt to taste

Combine the butter, rosemary leaves, garlic, lemon zest, lemon juice, red pepper flakes and salt in a bowl and mix well. Chill, covered, until serving time. Makes $^1/2$ cup.

Easy to prepare, flavored butters can add some variety to vegetables or grilled meats and fish. After making homemade breads or muffins, why settle for plain old butter?

Strawberry Blossoms

36 large strawberries
1 (8-ounce) package cream cheese, softened
6 tablespoons confectioners' sugar
3 tablespoons sour cream

Slice the stem from each strawberry to form a flat base. Slice each strawberry almost in half, to within $1/4$ inch of the base. Slice each half into 3 parts, also to within $1/4$ inch of the base. Pull the strawberry "petals" apart slightly. Combine the cream cheese, confectioners' sugar and sour cream in a bowl and beat until fluffy. Spoon into a pastry bag fitted with a star tip. Pipe the cream cheese mixture into the strawberries. Makes 36 servings.

Note: *If you don't have a pastry bag, spoon the cream cheese filling into a sealable plastic bag. Cut about $1/4$ inch from 1 corner of the bag and pipe the mixture into the strawberries. This method has the added advantage of no pastry bag to wash.*

74

Brunch & Breads

Spiced Pineapple

1 fresh pineapple, peeled, cored,
cut into 1/2-inch slices
2 tablespoons butter, melted
2 tablespoons bourbon or apple cider
1/4 cup firmly packed brown sugar
1/2 teaspoon freshly ground pepper

Place the pineapple slices in a single layer in a greased 9×13-inch baking dish. Drizzle with the butter and bourbon. Sprinkle with the brown sugar and pepper. Bake at 350 degrees for 25 to 30 minutes. Makes 6 servings.

Hot Gingered Fruit

1 (20-ounce) can sliced pineapple
1 (29-ounce) can cling peach halves, drained
2 (16-ounce) cans apricot halves, drained
1 (29-ounce) can pear halves, drained
10 maraschino cherries
3/4 cup firmly packed light brown sugar
1/4 cup (1/2 stick) butter, melted
1/2 teaspoon ginger

Drain the pineapple, reserving 2 tablespoons of the juice. Combine the pineapple, peaches, apricots and pears in a 2-quart casserole dish. Top with the cherries. Combine the reserved pineapple juice, brown sugar, butter, and ginger in a saucepan. Cook over low heat until the sugar dissolves. Pour over the fruit. Bake at 325 degrees for 40 minutes. Makes 12 servings.

Chapter Recipes

Entrées

Lobster-Filled Beef Tenderloin

3 lobster tails
1 (4- to 6-pound) beef tenderloin
1 tablespoon butter, melted
Garlic powder to taste
Salt and pepper to taste
Bacon slices

Place the lobster tails in boiling water in a saucepan and simmer for 5 minutes; drain. Remove the lobster meat from the shell in 1 piece. Trim the tip ends of the beef tenderloin. Cut a pocket by slicing lengthwise through the beef to within $^1/_2$ inch of the bottom, leaving $^1/_2$ inch uncut on both ends. Place the lobster tails end to end inside the beef. Split the lobster tails lengthwise if necessary to fill the entire length of the pocket. Drizzle with the butter. Truss the roast with twine at 2- to 3-inch intervals. Sprinkle with garlic powder, salt and pepper. Place the tenderloin on a rack in a roasting pan and top with several bacon slices. Roast at 425 degrees to 140 degrees on a meat thermometer for rare and 160 degrees for medium. Remove the bacon and twine. Cut the tenderloin into 10 slices. Makes 10 servings.

Note: *This dish is a real showstopper, but it's very easy to prepare.*

A Rest After Roasting

The "resting" of meats after roasting isn't just a snooty term that gastronomes employ to sound superior (don't worry, they have plenty of others to fall back on). It's true. Allowing a roast to sit at room temperature for even 5 or 10 minutes after leaving the oven allows any free-flowing juices an opportunity to retreat into the meat. Bottom line . . . you get a reputation for juicy meat.

Herb-Crusted Tenderloin with Red and Yellow Pepper Relish

1 tablespoon olive oil
2 (2¹/4- to 2³/4-pound) beef tenderloins, cut from thick end, trimmed
Salt and pepper to taste
6 tablespoons olive oil
6 garlic cloves, minced
2 tablespoons minced fresh thyme
2 tablespoons minced fresh rosemary
6 tablespoons Dijon mustard
Minced fresh thyme
Minced fresh rosemary
Red and Yellow Pepper Relish

Rub 1 tablespoon olive oil over the tenderloin. Sprinkle with salt and pepper. Cook the tenderloin over high heat in a nonstick skillet for 5 minutes or until brown on all sides. Place on a rack in a roasting pan. Combine 6 tablespoons olive oil, the garlic, 2 tablespoons thyme and 2 tablespoons rosemary in a small bowl. Spread the Dijon mustard over the top and sides of the tenderloin. Coat with the herb mixture. Roast at 375 degrees for 45 minutes or to 125 degrees on a meat thermometer for medium-rare. Remove the tenderloin to a serving dish. Let stand for 10 minutes. Cut into ¹/2-inch slices. Sprinkle with additional thyme and rosemary. Serve with Red and Yellow Pepper Relish. Makes 10 servings.

Red and Yellow Pepper Relish

1 large onion, thinly sliced
2 tablespoons butter
2 tablespoons olive oil
1 red bell pepper, coarsely chopped
1 yellow bell pepper, coarsely chopped
¹/3 cup pitted kalamata olives, coarsely chopped
1 tablespoon Dijon mustard
1 large garlic clove, chopped
Salt and pepper to taste

Sauté the onion in the butter and olive oil in a heavy skillet over medium-high heat for 5 minutes or until golden. Add the bell peppers and sauté for 3 minutes or just until tender. Add the olives, Dijon mustard and garlic. Cook for 1 minute, stirring constantly. Remove from the heat. Season with salt and pepper. Remove to a bowl and let cool. Chill, covered, for 10 hours or up to 2 days. Bring to room temperature before serving. Makes 2 cups.

Beef Tenderloin with Wine Sauce

1 (3- to 4-pound) beef tenderloin
Garlic powder to taste
Salt and pepper to taste
2 tablespoons butter
2 tablespoons Kitchen Bouquet
Wine Sauce or Mushroom Sauce

Place the tenderloin on a piece of heavy aluminum foil. Sprinkle both sides of the tenderloin with garlic powder, salt and pepper. Melt the butter with the Kitchen Bouquet in a small saucepan and brush over both sides of the tenderloin. Seal the foil around the meat. Chill for at least 8 hours. Let stand at room temperature for 1 hour before baking. Place the tenderloin in a roasting pan and roll back the foil to uncover the meat. Roast at 350 degrees to 140 degrees on a meat thermometer for rare and 160 degrees for medium. Serve with Wine Sauce or Mushroom Sauce. Makes 6 to 8 servings.

Note: *Double or triple this recipe as needed. This is a wonderful Christmas dinner dish because you can do all the preparations the day before.*

Wine Sauce

4 green onions, chopped
3 tablespoons unsalted butter
1/2 cup red wine or claret
1/2 cup beef consommé
2 teaspoons cornstarch
1/2 teaspoon lemon juice
1 jar mushrooms, drained (optional)

Sauté the green onions in the butter in a skillet for 1 minute. Stir in the red wine. Combine the beef consommé, cornstarch and lemon juice in a small bowl. Add to the green onion mixture and cook until thickened, stirring constantly. Add the mushrooms. Keep warm until serving time. Thin with the juices from the roast if desired. Makes 1 cup.

Mushroom Sauce

8 ounces fresh mushrooms
1 large or 2 small shallots
1/2 cup (1 stick) margarine
4 ounces tomato paste
3 tablespoons beef stock or soup base
(not bouillon)
3 tablespoons chives
1/2 teaspoon minced garlic
12 ounces port

Sauté the mushrooms and shallots in the margarine in a skillet over high heat until tender. Add the tomato paste, stock, chives, garlic and a little of the port. Stir until well blended. Add the remaining port and simmer for 30 minutes or until the liquid is reduced and the sauce is the desired consistency. Serve with beef or as a sauce over potatoes. Makes 4 servings.

Bulgogi
(Korean Barbecued Beef)

2 pounds sirloin steak or other lean beef
4 teaspoons chopped green onions
3 tablespoons sugar
1/4 cup soy sauce
3 tablespoons sesame oil
1 teaspoon sesame seeds
3/4 teaspoon garlic powder
1 teaspoon pepper

Slice the sirloin steak across the grain into 2- to 3-inch strips. Combine the green onions, sugar, soy sauce, sesame oil, sesame seeds, garlic powder and pepper in a shallow baking dish and mix well. Add the steak and marinate in the refrigerator for 8 to 10 hours or longer. Grill the steak over hot coals, oven-broil or panfry as desired. Makes 4 servings.

Note: *The marinade used for this beef is excellent for chicken as well.*

Ragout de Boeuf

3 pounds boneless stewing beef, cubed
2 tablespoons vegetable oil
1 cup chopped onion
1 cup chopped carrots
1 1/2 teaspoons salt
1 teaspoon basil
1/2 teaspoon crumbled rosemary
1/2 teaspoon thyme
1/4 teaspoon pepper
3 cups dry red wine
2 cups sliced carrots
18 small white onions
8 ounces mushrooms, sliced
2 tablespoons butter or margarine
2 tablespoons flour
2 tablespoons chopped parsley

Brown the beef on all sides in the oil in a Dutch oven. Remove the beef. Add the chopped onion and chopped carrots to the Dutch oven. Cook until tender. Add the beef, salt, basil, rosemary, thyme, pepper and wine. Bring to a boil. Reduce the heat and simmer for 1 1/2 to 2 hours. Add the sliced carrots and onions. Simmer for 15 minutes. Stir in the mushrooms. Cook for 15 minutes longer or until the beef and vegetables are fork-tender. Combine the butter and flour in a small bowl and stir to a paste consistency. Whisk a little of the stew liquid into the butter mixture; stir the butter mixture into the stew. Cook until the stew is thickened, stirring constantly. Sprinkle with chopped parsley. Serve with buttered noodles. Makes 4 servings.

Note: *This French version of beef stew is thickened with a mixture of butter and flour called a "beurre manié." This is a convenient way to both thicken and enrich a braised meat dish.*

Keeping Herbs on Hand

To keep most herbs fresh, wrap unwashed sprigs in a damp, wrung-out towel and refrigerate in a sealable plastic bag. Parsley and dill weed, however, keep longest when their stems are immersed in water. Wash fresh herbs just before using. To freeze fresh herbs, first wash and pat dry, then discard the stems. Place the leaves in a sealable plastic bag, press out the air, and tightly seal. They will keep frozen for up to four months. Fresh herbs may also be frozen in cube form. Purée them with a small amount of water and freeze in ice cube trays. Store the cubes in plastic bags and use to season soups, sauces, and beverages.

Classic Beef Stroganoff

1 pound tenderloin or sirloin steak
8 ounces mushrooms, stemmed, sliced
1 medium onion, minced ($1/2$ to $3/4$ cup)
2 tablespoons butter
1 (10-ounce) can condensed beef broth
2 tablespoons ketchup
1 small garlic clove, minced
1 teaspoon salt
3 tablespoons flour
1 cup dairy sour cream
3 to 4 cups hot cooked pasta
(bow tie or linguini) or rice

Slice the steak across the grain into $1/2$-inch-thick strips about $1^{1}/2$ inches long. Tenderize with a meat mallet if you are using the sirloin. Sauté the mushrooms and onion in the butter in a skillet until tender. Remove the vegetables to a bowl. Add the steak to the skillet. Sauté until light brown on both sides. Reserve $1/3$ cup of the broth. Add the remaining broth, ketchup, garlic and salt to the steak and simmer, covered, for 15 minutes. Combine the reserved broth and flour in a small bowl and mix well. Stir into the beef mixture. Add the mushroom mixture. Heat to a boil. Cook for 1 minute, stirring constantly. Reduce the heat and stir in the sour cream. Serve over pasta or rice. Makes 4 servings.

Note: *This is a good dish to make ahead and freeze for later use. Prepare up to adding the sour cream and freeze. Add the sour cream just before serving and heat gently.*

Green Peppercorn Steaks

1 cup chicken stock or canned low-salt broth
1 cup beef stock or canned unsalted broth
4 (1¹/2-inch-thick) beef fillets (8 ounces each)
Salt and freshly ground pepper to taste
2 tablespoons olive oil
1 tablespoon butter
2 tablespoons chopped shallots
1 tablespoon dried green peppercorns, crushed
¹/2 cup dry red wine vinegar
2 tablespoons Cognac
2 cups heavy cream
2¹/2 tablespoons freshly grated horseradish, or
2 tablespoons prepared horseradish

Bring the chicken stock and beef stock to a boil in a heavy saucepan. Reduce the heat and simmer for 15 minutes or until reduced to ¹/2 cup.

Season the beef fillets with salt and pepper. Sauté in the olive oil in a heavy skillet over medium-high heat, turning to brown both sides. Reduce the heat to medium. Cook for 5 minutes per side for medium-rare. Remove the fillets to a serving dish and keep warm.

Discard the oil in the skillet. Add the butter and stir over medium heat until melted. Add the shallots and peppercorns. Sauté for 5 minutes or until the shallots are golden brown. Stir in the vinegar and Cognac. Bring to a boil. Reduce the heat and simmer for 4 minutes or until reduced to ¹/4 cup. Stir in the reduced stock and cream. Cook for 5 minutes or until reduced to a thick sauce consistency, stirring occasionally. Fold in the horseradish. Season with salt. Spoon the sauce over the steaks.
Makes 4 servings.

Entrées

Fiesta Beef Casserole

1 pound ground beef
1 cup chopped onion
1 (10-ounce) can cream of chicken soup
1 (10-ounce) can tomatoes with green chiles
8 flour tortillas, torn into pieces
1 (15-ounce) can ranch-style beans
1 cup shredded cheese

Brown the beef and onion in a skillet, stirring until the beef is crumbly; drain. Purée the soup and tomatoes with green chiles in a blender. Layer the tortilla pieces, beef mixture, beans, soup mixture and cheese 1/2 at a time in a baking dish. Bake at 350 degrees for 30 minutes. Makes 6 to 8 servings.

Meat Loaf

2 large onions, finely chopped
2 garlic cloves, minced
3 tablespoons olive oil
1 1/2 pounds ground chuck
1 1/2 pounds ground pork
1 (8-ounce) can tomato sauce
1 cup plain bread crumbs
1 egg
2 tablespoons horseradish sauce
Salt and freshly ground pepper to taste
3 tablespoons ketchup

Sauté the onions and garlic in the olive oil in a skillet over low heat for 15 minutes or until the onions are translucent. Let cool. Combine the ground chuck, ground pork, tomato sauce, bread crumbs, egg, horseradish sauce, salt, pepper and 1/2 of the onion mixture in a large bowl and stir just until mixed. Pack lightly into a 3×7-inch loaf pan. Round the top to form a crown. Top with the remaining onion mixture and drizzle with the ketchup. Bake at 350 degrees for 45 to 60 minutes. Let stand for 15 minutes before serving. Makes 6 to 8 servings.

Pork Loin with Caramelized Onions

1 (3- to 4-pound) pork loin roast,
split in half lengthwise
Garlic cloves, sliced
Fresh rosemary
Kosher salt
Freshly ground pepper
Caramelized Onions

Spread the pork loin halves with a generous amount of garlic and rosemary. Sprinkle lightly with kosher salt and pepper. Tie the loin halves together with twine and wrap in plastic wrap. Chill for 12 hours. Place the roast in an oiled roasting pan. Bake, uncovered, at 500 degrees for 55 minutes or to 140 to 150 degrees on a meat thermometer. Let stand for 15 minutes before serving. Serve with Caramelized Onions. Makes 8 to 10 servings.

Caramelized Onions

8 small red or Vidalia onions
1/2 cup (1 stick) butter
1 bunch fresh thyme
4 large garlic cloves, each cut into 4 slivers
Salt and pepper to taste
1 1/2 cups balsamic vinegar
1 1/2 cups red wine

Trim the bottom of each onion to make a flat base. Cut a cross halfway through each onion. Core the onions, leaving the bottoms intact. Combine the butter and thyme in a small bowl and mix well. Stuff each onion with 2 of the garlic slivers and 1 tablespoon of the butter mixture. Place the onions in a roasting pan. Sprinkle with salt and pepper. Drizzle 1/2 of the vinegar and 1/2 of the wine over the onions. Bake at 350 degrees for 1 hour or until the onions are tender, basting frequently with the pan juices. Reduce the heat to 300 degrees. Add the remaining vinegar and wine. Cook for 1 hour longer or until the onions are crispy and caramelized on the outside and tender on the inside. Top the onions with the thick pan sauce to serve.

Crumb-Coated Pork Tenderloin

1½ pounds pork tenderloin
3 tablespoons olive oil
½ cup dry bread crumbs
⅓ cup chopped fresh basil
3 tablespoons chopped fresh thyme
1 tablespoon freshly ground pepper

Coat the tenderloin with the olive oil. Combine the bread crumbs, basil, thyme and pepper in a small bowl and mix well. Press the crumb mixture over the tenderloin. Place on a rack in a roasting pan. Bake at 425 degrees for 25 to 30 minutes or to 160 degrees on a meat thermometer. Let stand for 10 minutes before slicing. Makes 4 to 6 servings.

Note: *This is a great company recipe that takes very little effort.*

Loin of Pork in Red Wine

1 (3- to 4-pound) pork loin roast
Salt and pepper to taste
Sage to taste
Nutmeg to taste
2 tablespoons vegetable oil
1 garlic clove, pressed
¼ cup chopped onion
¼ cup chopped fresh parsley
1 bay leaf
2 cups red wine
1 cup beef consommé

Rub the pork roast with salt, pepper, sage and nutmeg. Heat the oil with the garlic in a skillet over medium-high heat. Add the pork roast and brown on all sides. Place in a roasting pan. Add the onion, parsley, bay leaf and wine. Bake at 350 degrees for 2 hours, turning the roast twice during the baking. Add the beef consommé. Bake for 20 minutes longer. Remove to a serving dish. Heat the pan drippings, scraping all the browned bits into the sauce. Serve with the pork. Makes 8 to 10 servings.

Note: *This pork roast will melt in your mouth. Everyone loves it—kids and company!*

Pesto Pork Chops

The filling
3 tablespoons crumbled feta cheese
2 tablespoons refrigerated pesto
1 tablespoon pine nuts, toasted

For the filling, combine the cheese, pesto and pine nuts in a small bowl and mix well.

The glaze
2 tablespoons jalapeño chile jelly
2 to 3 tablespoons refrigerated pesto
1 tablespoon balsamic vinegar

For the glaze, melt the jelly in a small saucepan over low heat. Stir in the pesto and vinegar and heat through.

The rub
1 teaspoon minced garlic
1 teaspoon freshly ground black pepper
$1/2$ teaspoon cayenne pepper
$1/2$ teaspoon celery seeds
$1/2$ teaspoon fennel seeds, crushed
$1/4$ teaspoon thyme
$1/4$ teaspoon cumin

For the rub, combine the garlic, black pepper, cayenne pepper, celery seeds, fennel seeds, thyme and cumin in a small bowl and mix well.

The pork chops
4 ($1^{1}/4$-inch-thick) pork loin chops with pockets
Fresh basil leaves (optional)

For the pork chops, spoon the filling into the pockets. Secure with wooden picks. Coat all sides evenly with the rub. Arrange heated coals around a drip pan in a covered grill. Place the chops on the grill rack over the drip pan. Grill, covered, for 35 to 40 minutes or until the juices run clear, turning once and brushing with the glaze during the last 10 minutes of grilling. Garnish with basil leaves. Makes 4 servings.

Grilled Pork Chops

1/2 cup soy sauce
1 1/2 tablespoons sugar
2 1/2 tablespoons firmly packed brown sugar
1 tablespoon tarragon vinegar
1 tablespoon ginger
1 garlic clove, minced
4 boneless butterflied pork chops

Combine the soy sauce, sugar, brown sugar, vinegar, ginger and garlic in a glass baking dish large enough to hold the pork chops in a single layer. Add the pork chops and marinate in the refrigerator for 8 to 10 hours, turning once. Grill the pork chops over hot coals until cooked through or to 170 degrees on a meat thermometer. Makes 4 servings.

Note: *If you have trouble finding tarragon vinegar, try a white wine vinegar or other light vinegar and add some dried tarragon.*

Saucy Ham Loaves

3 cups (1 1/2 pounds) ground ham
2 cups (1 pound) ground pork
1 cup saltine cracker crumbs
2 eggs, lightly beaten
1/2 cup milk
1 tablespoon minced onion
1/2 teaspoon dry mustard
1/2 teaspoon Worcestershire sauce
1/4 teaspoon pepper
1 cup firmly packed brown sugar
1/4 cup water
1/3 cup white vinegar
1 3/4 teaspoons prepared mustard

Combine the ham, pork, cracker crumbs, eggs, milk, onion, dry mustard, Worcestershire sauce and pepper in a large bowl and mix well. Shape into 8 to 10 loaves. Arrange the loaves in a 9×13-inch baking dish. Combine the brown sugar, water, vinegar and prepared mustard in a saucepan. Bring to a boil. Reduce the heat and simmer for 2 minutes, stirring constantly. Bake the ham loaves at 300 degrees for 1 1/2 to 2 hours, basting every 15 minutes with the brown sugar mixture. Makes 8 to 10 servings.

Note: *This is a great way to use leftover spiral-cut ham. If you have any extra loaves, freeze them with a little of the basting sauce in sealable plastic freezer bags.*

Orange-Roasted Cornish Game Hens with Cherry Sauce

4 Cornish game hens
Salt and pepper to taste
3/4 cup frozen orange juice concentrate, thawed
1/2 cup marmalade
Cherry Sauce

Season the game hens with salt and pepper. Combine the orange juice concentrate and marmalade in a bowl and mix well. Bake the game hens on a rack in a roasting pan at 350 degrees for 20 minutes per pound. Increase the heat to 425 degrees. Cook for 30 minutes longer, basting the game hens every 10 minutes with the orange juice mixture. Serve with Cherry Sauce. Makes 4 servings.

Cherry Sauce

2 (8-ounce) cans pitted black cherries in syrup
1/2 cup burgundy or other red wine
3 tablespoons firmly packed brown sugar
2 tablespoons cornstarch

Purée 1 can of the cherries with the wine in a blender. Combine the puréed cherries with the remaining can of cherries, brown sugar and cornstarch in a small saucepan and mix well. Bring to a boil. Reduce the heat and simmer until thickened, stirring constantly. Makes 2 cups.

Note: *Try this hot cherry sauce over vanilla ice cream.*

Brining

Professional chefs know that brining, the process of soaking a whole chicken or turkey in a salt-water solution before roasting, helps retain much of the moisture in the finished bird.

Broccoli and Chicken Alfredo

1 bunch broccoli, cut into florets
2 garlic cloves, pressed
3 tablespoons vegetable oil
4 whole boneless skinless
chicken breasts, cubed
8 ounces spinach fettuccini
1/2 cup (1 stick) butter
1 cup light cream
3/4 cup (3 ounces) grated Parmesan cheese
1 cup (4 ounces) mozzarella cheese

Steam the broccoli for 5 minutes or until tender-crisp; drain. Sauté the garlic in the oil in a skillet for 1 minute. Add the chicken. Cook until tender, stirring constantly. Prepare the fettuccini using the package directions; drain. Melt the butter in a large saucepan. Add the broccoli, chicken, fettuccini, cream and Parmesan cheese. Cook until heated through, stirring constantly. Pour into a greased 9×13-inch baking dish. Top with the mozzarella cheese. Bake at 350 degrees for 15 to 20 minutes or until heated through. Makes 8 servings.

Hot Chicken Salad

1 cup chopped celery
1 tablespoon butter
2 chicken breasts, cooked, chopped
1 cup rice, cooked
1 (10-ounce) can cream of chicken soup
3/4 cup mayonnaise
1 teaspoon minced onion
1 teaspoon lemon juice
1 teaspoon salt
1/2 cup sliced water chestnuts
1/2 cup slivered almonds
1 cup crushed cornflakes

Sauté the celery in the butter in a skillet until the celery is tender. Combine the celery, chicken and rice in a large bowl. Blend the soup, mayonnaise, onion, lemon juice and salt together in a bowl and add to the chicken mixture. Stir in the water chestnuts. Spoon into a greased 2-quart baking dish. Sprinkle with the almonds and cornflakes. Bake at 350 degrees for 30 minutes. Makes 8 servings.

Mexican Chicken Rolls

8 boneless skinless chicken breasts
8 slices Monterey Jack cheese
1 large can whole green chiles
2/3 cup bread crumbs
1/2 cup (2 ounces) grated Parmesan cheese
1 1/2 tablespoons chili powder
1/2 teaspoon cumin
1/2 teaspoon salt
1/4 teaspoon pepper
6 tablespoons butter, melted
32 ounces tomato sauce
1/3 cup sliced green onions
1/2 teaspoon cumin
Salt and pepper to taste
Tabasco sauce to taste

Pound the chicken breasts into a 1/4-inch thickness. Place 1 slice Monterey Jack cheese and 1 whole green chile on each chicken breast and roll up to enclose the filling. Combine the bread crumbs, Parmesan cheese, chili powder, 1/2 teaspoon cumin, 1/2 teaspoon salt and 1/4 teaspoon pepper in a shallow dish. Dip each chicken breast roll in the butter. Coat with the bread crumb mixture. Chill, covered, for 8 to 10 hours. Combine the tomato sauce, green onions, 1/2 teaspoon cumin, salt and pepper to taste and Tabasco sauce in a bowl and mix well. Pour over the chicken in a baking dish. Bake at 350 degrees for 35 to 40 minutes. Makes 8 servings.

Seay Mansion Society Luncheon Chicken

1/2 cup (1 stick) butter
12 boneless skinless chicken breasts
Salt, pepper, garlic salt and MSG to taste
2 cups sour cream
2 (10-ounce) cans cream of asparagus or cream of celery soup
8 ounces mushrooms, sliced
1 cup (4 ounces) shredded Cheddar cheese
1 (10-ounce) package frozen asparagus

Melt the butter in a 9×13-inch baking dish. Season the chicken with salt, pepper, garlic salt and MSG and arrange in the pan. Combine the sour cream, soup and mushrooms in a bowl. Spread 1/4 of the soup mixture over the chicken. Sprinkle with 1/2 of the cheese. Layer the asparagus, the remaining soup mixture and the remaining cheese over the cheese. Chill, covered, for 8 to 10 hours. Bake, covered, at 350 degrees for 1 hour. Makes 12 servings.

Lemon Chicken

The sauce

1/2 cup lemon juice
1/4 cup vegetable oil
2 tablespoons grated lemon zest
1 tablespoon soy sauce
1 garlic clove, pressed
1/2 teaspoon salt
1/2 teaspoon pepper

For the sauce, combine the lemon juice, oil, lemon zest, soy sauce, garlic, salt and pepper in a bowl and mix well. Chill for at least 1 hour.

The chicken

1/2 cup flour
1 teaspoon salt
1/2 teaspoon pepper
2 teaspoons paprika
6 boneless skinless chicken breasts
1/2 cup (1 stick) butter, melted

For the chicken, combine the flour, salt, pepper and paprika in a shallow bowl. Dip the chicken in the flour mixture. Arrange the chicken in a single layer in a baking pan. Brush the butter over the chicken. Bake at 400 degrees for 30 minutes. Turn the chicken. Pour the sauce over the chicken. Bake for 30 minutes longer or until golden brown and tender. Makes 6 servings.

Chicken Marinade

1 cup olive oil
1/2 cup white wine vinegar
6 green onions, chopped
1 tablespoon tarragon
1 teaspoon salt
1 teaspoon freshly ground pepper

Combine the olive oil, vinegar, green onions, tarragon, salt and pepper in a shallow baking dish. Marinate chicken halves in the mixture for 2 to 3 hours, turning frequently. Grill or broil the chicken, basting frequently with the marinade. Makes 1 1/2 cups.

Chicken and Vegetable Tetrazzini

1/2 cup (1 stick) butter
2/3 cup flour
1 quart milk
8 ounces Velveeta cheese
2 cups (8 ounces) shredded Cheddar cheese
Salt and pepper to taste
1 (16-ounce) package linguini
Fresh vegetables, chopped, lightly steamed
(carrots, red bell pepper, asparagus,
broccoli, mushrooms, onion, etc.)
Frozen peas and corn
4 grilled chicken breasts, cut into strips
or cubes
Fresh bread crumbs

Melt the butter in a heavy saucepan. Whisk in the flour. Cook over low heat for 5 minutes or until thickened, stirring constantly. Whisk in the milk, Velveeta cheese and Cheddar cheese until smooth and thickened. Season with salt and pepper.

Cook the linguini using the package directions; drain. Combine the pasta, fresh and frozen vegetables and sauce in a large bowl and stir well. Fold in the chicken. Spoon into a greased 9×13-inch baking dish. Top with bread crumbs. Bake, covered, at 325 degrees for 1 1/4 hours. Let stand for 5 to 10 minutes. Makes 10 to 12 servings.

Andrews Park

This Norman city park was formally established in the early 1890s and is home to Assistance League of Norman's annual May Fair Arts Festival. Using the New Deal programs of the 1930s, the park was improved by the construction of an amphitheater, wading pool, and bath houses. The WPA amphitheater is a highlight of the park's New Deal resources. Built from native stone with a compatible rose-colored concrete cap, the structure is home to many local events and performances. Andrews Park was placed on the National Register of Historic Places in 2000.

Cheesy Chile Chicken

4 chicken breasts, cooked, boned, chopped
1/4 cup chopped green chiles
2 cups (8 ounces) shredded Cheddar cheese
8 ounces fresh mushrooms, sliced
1 large can black olives, chopped
1 bunch green onions, chopped
1 (10-ounce) can cream of mushroom soup
2 cups sour cream
1 (8-ounce) package cream cheese, softened
1 cup milk
12 flour tortillas
2 cups (8 ounces) shredded Cheddar cheese
1 cup crushed potato chips

Combine the chicken, green chiles, 2 cups Cheddar cheese, mushrooms, olives and green onions in a large bowl and mix well. Whisk the soup, sour cream, cream cheese and milk together in a bowl. Add to the chicken mixture and stir until well combined. Place 4 tortillas in the bottom of a greased 9×13-inch baking dish. Spread 1/3 of the chicken mixture over the tortillas. Continue layering the remaining tortillas and chicken mixture. Top with 2 cups Cheddar cheese and the potato chips. Bake at 350 degrees for 30 minutes. Makes 8 to 10 servings.

Chicken Rice Casserole

1 package wild rice mix
1 can French-style green beans, drained
1 (10-ounce) can cream of celery soup
1/2 cup mayonnaise
1 small package slivered almonds
1 can sliced water chestnuts, drained
1/4 cup grated onion
1 small jar pimento
2 to 3 cups chopped cooked chicken
Salt and pepper to taste
Shredded sharp cheese

Prepare the wild rice mix using the package directions, but undercook slightly. Combine the cooked rice, green beans, soup, mayonnaise, almonds, water chestnuts, onion, pimento, chicken, salt and pepper in a bowl and mix well. Spoon into a buttered 3-quart casserole dish. Sprinkle with cheese. Bake at 350 degrees for 30 minutes or until bubbly. Makes 8 servings.

Chicken Cara Mia

4 large chicken breasts
3/4 teaspoon seasoned salt
1 (6-ounce) jar marinated artichoke hearts
1 tablespoon flour
1/2 cup water
1/4 cup (or more) dry white wine
1 chicken bouillon cube, crumbled
12 small mushrooms, sliced
Hot cooked noodles
1 tablespoon chopped fresh parsley

Sprinkle the chicken breasts with the seasoned salt. Drain the artichokes, reserving the marinade. Heat the marinade in a skillet. Add the chicken. Cook over low heat until brown on both sides. Remove the chicken. Add the flour, water, wine and bouillon cube. Cook until the mixture boils and thickens, stirring constantly. Add the artichokes and mushrooms. Nestle the chicken breasts in the skillet, spooning the sauce over the chicken. Simmer, covered, over low heat for 20 minutes or until the chicken is tender. Serve over hot cooked noodles. Sprinkle with the parsley. Makes 4 servings.

Note: *You may find it convenient to prepare this dish in an electric skillet.*

The Best Chicken Broth

Many soups begin with a base of chicken broth. While canned broths are a great substitute when you are in a hurry, nothing will improve the taste of your soup more than your own homemade chicken stock. Make it ahead and store it in your freezer so it will be ready when you are. This is a good basic recipe.

Rinse 1 (4- to 5-pound) hen and pat dry. Season the chicken with salt and freshly ground pepper to taste. Combine the chicken, 3 cups chopped yellow onions, 1 1/2 cups chopped carrots, 1/2 cup chopped celery, 2 chopped seeded fresh jalapeño chiles, 6 garlic cloves, 3 bay leaves, 4 sprigs of fresh thyme and enough water to cover the chicken in a soup pot. Bring to a boil. Reduce the heat and simmer, uncovered, for 2 hours or until the meat is very tender and separating from the bones. Skim off the foam that rises to the surface during the cooking. Let stand for 20 minutes. Remove the chicken from the bones, discarding the skin and bones. Strain the stock and freeze in small containers. Makes 4 to 6 cups.

Chicken Valentino

2 tablespoons flour
$^1/_2$ teaspoon tarragon or oregano
1 teaspoon each salt and paprika
$^1/_4$ teaspoon pepper
3 chicken breasts
2 medium garlic cloves, minced
2 tablespoons butter
1 tablespoon vegetable oil
$^1/_2$ cup dry white wine
$^1/_4$ cup orange juice
$^1/_2$ cup white grapes
Orange slices

Combine the flour, tarragon, salt, paprika and pepper in a paper bag. Add the chicken breasts 1 at a time and shake well. Sauté the garlic in the butter and oil in a skillet over medium-low heat for 1 minute. Add the chicken. Cook until both sides are brown, turning once. Stir in the wine and orange juice. Cook, covered, over low heat for 25 minutes or until the chicken is tender. Add the grapes. Cook for 5 minutes longer. Garnish with orange slices. Serve with white, brown or wild rice. Makes 3 servings.

Chicken Piccata

6 boneless skinless chicken breasts
2 cups flour
$1^1/_2$ teaspoons salt
$^3/_4$ teaspoon pepper
$1^1/_2$ teaspoons garlic powder
9 tablespoons olive oil
$1^1/_2$ cups white wine
1 cup (4 ounces) freshly grated Parmesan cheese
6 tablespoons butter, melted
3 tablespoons lemon juice
$1^1/_2$ tablespoons chopped fresh parsley
$1^1/_2$ teaspoons paprika

Pound the chicken into a $^1/_4$-inch thickness. Combine the flour, salt, pepper and garlic powder in a paper bag. Add the chicken breasts 1 at a time and shake well. Heat the olive oil in a skillet to 325 degrees. Sauté the chicken in the oil until brown on both sides. Stir in the wine. Bring to a boil. Reduce the heat and simmer until the chicken is tender. Top with the cheese. Broil for 3 minutes. Combine the butter and lemon juice in a bowl and drizzle over the chicken. Sprinkle with the parsley and paprika. Makes 6 servings.

Broiled Greek Chicken

4 to 6 boneless skinless chicken breasts
1 cup plain yogurt
4 to 6 garlic cloves, pressed
1/2 teaspoon oregano
1/4 teaspoon pepper
Fresh lemon juice to taste
1 cup (4 ounces) crumbled feta cheese
Yogurt Sauce

Pound the chicken breasts into a 1/4-inch thickness. Combine the yogurt, garlic, oregano and pepper in a shallow dish and mix well. Add the chicken and marinate for 1 hour. Broil the chicken on 1 side for 6 minutes. Sprinkle with lemon juice. Turn the chicken and sprinkle with the cheese. Broil for 8 to 10 minutes longer or until brown. Serve with Yogurt Sauce. Makes 4 to 6 servings.

Yogurt Sauce

2 cups plain yogurt
1/2 cup light or nonfat sour cream
2 teaspoons dehydrated onion
2 teaspoons fresh lemon juice
1 1/2 teaspoons dill weed
Salt and pepper to taste

Combine the yogurt, sour cream, onion, lemon juice, dill weed, salt and pepper in a small bowl and mix well. Makes 2 1/2 cups.

98

Entrées

Southwest Chicken Wraps

2 to 4 pepperoncini, chopped
1 medium red onion, chopped
1 tablespoon chili powder
1 tablespoon safflower oil
3 cups shredded cooked chicken breast
1 package frozen phyllo dough, thawed
1 cup (4 ounces) shredded Cheddar cheese
3/4 cup (1 1/2 sticks) margarine, melted

Cook the pepperoncini, onion and chili powder in the safflower oil in a skillet over medium heat until the onion is tender. Add the chicken and stir well. Let stand until cool.

Unroll the phyllo and cover it with waxed paper covered with a damp towel. Keep the unused portion covered until needed. Brush 2 sheets of the phyllo with the margarine. Layer the dough 2 sheets at a time with the margarine to make 5 double layers, using 1/2 of the phyllo. Cut the layers in half lengthwise and crosswise to form 4 rectangles. Spoon 1/2 cup of the chicken mixture on the long edge of each rectangle. Sprinkle each with 2 tablespoons of the cheese. Fold in the short edges over the filling. Roll up tightly from the long edge. Place the rolls seam side down in a greased 9×13-inch baking dish. Brush the tops with the margarine. Repeat the procedure with the remaining phyllo and chicken mixture. Bake at 400 degrees for 10 minutes or until golden. Serve with picante sauce and sour cream. Makes 8 servings.

99
Entrées

Chinese Chicken Sundaes

The marinated chicken

$^1/_2$ cup soy sauce
$^1/_2$ cup pineapple juice
$^1/_4$ cup vegetable oil
1 teaspoon dry mustard
1 teaspoon ginger
$^1/_4$ teaspoon pepper
5 whole chicken breasts, cooked, boned,
sliced into flat strips

For the marinated chicken, combine the soy sauce, pineapple juice, oil, dry mustard, ginger and pepper in a shallow dish. Add the chicken strips. Marinate in the refrigerator for 24 hours. Heat the chicken in the marinade before serving.

The gravy
2 (10-ounce) cans cream of mushroom soup
1 cup milk

For the gravy, whisk the soup and milk together in a saucepan. Cook over low heat until heated through.

The sundaes
Hot cooked rice
Chinese noodles
2 cups chopped tomatoes
2 cups (8 ounces) shredded cheese
2 cups chopped celery
1 bunch green onions, chopped
2 cans pineapple tidbits
1 small package coconut
1 small package slivered almonds

For the sundaes, place 3 scoops of hot cooked rice in a banana split boat using an ice cream scoop. Top with some of the chicken strips. Top with some of the warm gravy and your choice of Chinese noodles, tomatoes, cheese, celery, green onions, pineapple tidbits, coconut and almonds. Makes 10 servings.

Roast Racks of Lamb

2 racks of lamb, trimmed
Salt and pepper to taste
1 tablespoon olive oil
1 egg
2 tablespoons Dijon mustard
3 garlic cloves, minced
1 cup walnuts or pecans
2 tablespoons rosemary
2 tablespoons grated Parmesan cheese
1/2 teaspoon garlic powder

Season the lamb with salt and pepper. Sear the lamb in the olive oil in a skillet over high heat until brown on all sides. Beat the egg with the Dijon mustard and garlic in a bowl. Combine the walnuts, rosemary, cheese and garlic powder in a food processor and process until crumbly. Spread the mustard mixture over the lamb. Coat with the walnut mixture. Place the lamb on a rack in a roasting pan. Bake at 425 degrees for 20 minutes or to the desired temperature. Makes 6 servings.

Note: *This flavorful coating works well with leg of lamb.*

Lemon Grilled Lamb Chops

1/2 cup Dijon mustard
1/2 cup fresh lemon juice
6 tablespoons balsamic vinegar
3 tablespoons chopped fresh thyme
1 teaspoon pepper
2/3 cup extra-virgin olive oil
24 lamb rib chops or loin chops
Salt to taste
1 lemon, halved
Fresh thyme sprigs (optional)
Lemon wedges (optional)

Combine the Dijon mustard, lemon juice, vinegar, chopped thyme and pepper in a bowl and mix well. Whisk in the olive oil gradually. Divide the mixture between 2 large shallow baking dishes. Arrange 12 of the chops in each dish in a single layer. Turn to coat with the mustard mixture. Marinate, covered, in the refrigerator for 2 to 4 hours. Grill over hot coals for 7 minutes on each side for medium-rare. Remove to a serving platter. Sprinkle with salt. Squeeze the lemon halves over the lamb. Garnish with fresh thyme sprigs and lemon wedges. Makes 8 servings.

Braised Lamb Shanks

6 lamb shanks
Salt and pepper to taste
2 tablespoons butter
1 tablespoon butter
1 (15-ounce) can white onions
12 medium mushrooms, sliced
4 shallots, or 1 small onion, chopped
1 garlic clove, quartered
1/2 cup burgundy
2 medium tomatoes, peeled, diced
2 tablespoons flour (optional)
2 tablespoons butter, softened
Chopped fresh parsley

Season the lamb with salt and pepper. Brown the shanks in 2 tablespoons butter in a Dutch oven. Remove the shanks and add 1 tablespoon butter to the Dutch oven. Drain the white onions, reserving 1/2 cup of the liquid. Add the white onions, mushrooms, shallots and garlic to the Dutch oven. Sauté until golden brown. Add the shanks, wine and reserved onion liquid. Bring to a boil. Reduce the heat and simmer, covered, for 1 1/2 hours, turning the shanks occasionally. Stir in the tomatoes. Simmer for 30 minutes longer or until the shanks are fork-tender. Remove the shanks to a heated platter. Combine the flour and 2 tablespoons butter in a small bowl and mix well. Stir into the sauce. Cook over medium heat for 1 minute or until the sauce is thickened. Pour over the shanks. Sprinkle with parsley. Serve with hot cooked noodles or with a long grain and wild rice mixture. Makes 6 servings.

Lamb Dijon

3 single racks of lamb, trimmed
3 tablespoons Dijon mustard
1/3 cup olive oil
2 garlic cloves, minced
1 tablespoon salt
1 1/2 cups dry red wine
2 tablespoons honey

Coat the lamb with a mixture of the Dijon mustard, olive oil and garlic. Let stand for several hours. Roast at 375 degrees for 40 minutes, basting with the wine and honey. Serve the pan juices with the lamb. Makes 10 servings.

Veal Scaloppine

$^1/4$ cup flour
$^1/2$ cup (2 ounces) grated Parmesan cheese
1 teaspoon salt
$^1/8$ teaspoon pepper
$1^1/2$ pounds ($^1/4$-inch) veal cutlets
2 tablespoons olive oil
1 garlic clove
$^1/2$ cup dry white wine
$^1/2$ cup consommé or stock
1 tablespoon lemon juice
Chopped fresh parsley

Combine the flour, cheese, salt and pepper in a small bowl and sprinkle over the veal cutlets. Pound the flour mixture into both sides of the veal using the smooth side of a meat mallet. Heat the olive oil and garlic in a skillet. Add the veal cutlets. Cook until light brown on both sides. Discard the garlic. Stir in the wine, consommé and lemon juice. Simmer, covered, over low heat for 30 minutes. Sprinkle with parsley. Makes 6 servings.

Port and Peppercorn Veal Scallops

8 veal scallops (about 1 pound)
Salt to taste
$^1/4$ cup flour
2 tablespoons unsalted butter
2 tablespoons olive oil
$^1/2$ cup port
1 tablespoon green peppercorns,
packed in brine, drained

Pound the veal lightly. Sprinkle with salt and coat with the flour. Brown the veal in the butter and olive oil in a skillet. Remove the veal and discard the fat. Add the port to the skillet. Bring to a boil, scraping up the browned bits. Cook for 1 minute or until reduced by $^1/2$. Stir in the peppercorns. Pour over the veal. Serve immediately. Makes 8 servings.

Veal Parmesan

1¹/2 pounds (¹/2-inch) veal cutlets,
cut into medallions
2 eggs
¹/4 cup water
¹/2 teaspoon salt
¹/4 teaspoon pepper
1 cup dry bread crumbs
¹/2 cup (2 ounces) grated Parmesan cheese
1 tablespoon parsley flakes
¹/2 teaspoon salt
¹/4 teaspoon pepper
¹/2 cup vegetable oil
Marinara Sauce
¹/2 cup (2 ounces) grated Parmesan cheese
2 cups (8 ounces) shredded mozzarella cheese

Pound the veal medallions ¹/8 inch thick between sheets of waxed paper. Beat the eggs with the water, ¹/2 teaspoon salt and ¹/4 teaspoon pepper in a shallow bowl. Combine the bread crumbs, ¹/2 cup Parmesan cheese, parsley flakes, ¹/2 teaspoon salt and ¹/4 teaspoon pepper on a plate. Dip each medallion in the egg mixture; coat with the bread crumb mixture, pressing the crumbs firmly into the medallions. Let dry on waxed paper. Sauté the medallions in the oil in a skillet for 2 to 3 minutes on each side or until golden brown. Arrange in a baking dish coated with nonstick cooking spray. Spoon Marinara Sauce over the veal. Sprinkle with ¹/2 cup Parmesan cheese and the mozzarella cheese. Bake, covered, at 350 degrees for 45 minutes. Makes 8 to 10 servings.

Marinara Sauce

2 (15-ounce) cans tomatoes
1 (6-ounce) can tomato paste
¹/2 cup water
2 garlic cloves, minced
1 teaspoon basil
1 teaspoon oregano
¹/2 teaspoon salt
¹/4 teaspoon pepper

Purée the tomatoes in a blender or food processor. Combine the tomatoes, tomato paste, water, garlic, basil, oregano, salt and pepper in a saucepan. Bring to a boil. Reduce the heat and simmer for 1 hour, stirring frequently. Makes 4 cups.

Salmon en Papillote

1/4 cup reduced-fat cottage cheese

1 tablespoon prepared horseradish

1/2 teaspoon minced fresh parsley

12 ounces (1/2-inch) skinless salmon fillet, cut into 4 pieces

Lemon pepper to taste

2 small zucchini, cut diagonally into 1/4-inch slices

2 small yellow squash, cut diagonally into 1/4-inch slices

4 carrots, julienned, cut into 1 1/2-inch-long pieces

Combine the cottage cheese and horseradish in a food processor and process until smooth. Remove to a bowl and stir in the parsley. Chill, covered, until serving time. Cut sheets of parchment paper into 4 large squares. Fold each square in half; trim into large heart shapes. Open the paper hearts. Place 1 piece of salmon on 1 side of each heart. Sprinkle with lemon pepper. Layer the zucchini, yellow squash and carrots over the salmon. Sprinkle with more lemon pepper if desired.

For each packet, fold the empty side of the paper heart over the fish and vegetables and align the edges. Make a small fold at the top edge, then repeat to make a double seal. Continue creasing and making a double seal around the entire edge. Twist the parchment at the pointed end to hold the folds in place. Check to be sure the edges are tightly sealed. Place the packets on a large baking sheet. Bake at 400 degrees for 20 minutes or until the paper is puffed and brown. Cut a large "x" in the top of each packet and fold back the points. Check to see if the fish flakes easily and the vegetables are tender-crisp. Reseal and bake for 3 minutes longer if necessary. Remove the packets to dinner plates and open the flaps. Serve with the chilled horseradish sauce and crusty bread. Makes 4 servings.

Tarragon Salmon

1/4 cup olive oil
1 tablespoon white wine vinegar
1 tablespoon Dijon mustard
1 teaspoon sugar
2 tablespoons chopped fresh parsley
1 tablespoon chopped fresh tarragon, or
1 teaspoon dried tarragon
4 salmon steaks
Lemon juice to taste
2 tablespoons olive oil

Combine 1/4 cup olive oil, the vinegar, Dijon mustard, sugar, parsley and tarragon in a small bowl and mix well. Brush the salmon with lemon juice and 2 tablespoons olive oil. Broil for 5 minutes on each side or until the salmon flakes easily. Serve with the tarragon mixture. Makes 4 servings.

Aïoli-Topped Grilled Tuna

1/4 cup olive oil
2 tablespoons red wine vinegar
2 tablespoons chopped fresh basil
2 teaspoons chopped fresh thyme
2 teaspoons tarragon
2 large garlic cloves, finely chopped
1/3 cup mayonnaise
4 (7-ounce) tuna steaks, cut 1 inch thick
Salt and pepper to taste

Whisk the olive oil, vinegar, basil, thyme, tarragon and garlic together in a shallow bowl. Reserve 1 1/2 tablespoons of the marinade. Combine the reserved marinade and mayonnaise in a small bowl. Sprinkle the fish with salt and pepper. Place in the marinade, turning to coat evenly. Marinate at room temperature for 1 hour, turning the fish occasionally. Grill over hot coals for 3 minutes on each side for medium. Top the fish with the aïoli (mayonnaise mixture). Makes 4 servings.

Is the Fish Done?

To test fish for doneness, prod it with a fork at its thickest point. A properly cooked fish is opaque, has milky white juices, and just begins to flake easily. Undercooked fish is translucent and has clear, watery juices.

Cheesy Fish Fillets

1 pound flounder or other fish fillets
1/2 teaspoon salt
Dash of pepper
2 tomatoes, peeled, sliced
Salt to taste
1/4 cup dry white wine
1/2 teaspoon basil
1/2 cup (2 ounces) shredded sharp American
or Parmesan cheese

Place the fillets in a greased 7×11-inch baking dish. Sprinkle with 1/2 teaspoon salt and the pepper. Top with the tomatoes and sprinkle with salt to taste. Drizzle the wine over the fish. Sprinkle with the basil. Bake at 350 degrees for 20 minutes. Top with the cheese. Bake for 5 to 10 minutes longer or until the fish flakes easily. Makes 4 to 5 servings.

Note: *This is a low-calorie dish and is bound to please even non-fish lovers.*

Fish with Tomatoes and Linguini

2 tablespoons olive oil
4 garlic cloves, minced
1 (15-ounce) can whole tomatoes
2 tablespoons chopped fresh basil leaves, or
2 teaspoons dried basil
2 teaspoons lemon juice
1/2 teaspoon salt
1/8 teaspoon pepper
1 pound flounder fillets
8 ounces linguini, cooked

Heat the olive oil in a skillet. Sauté the garlic in the oil until golden. Stir in the tomatoes, basil, lemon juice, salt and pepper. Cook for 5 minutes, stirring occasionally. Arrange the fillets on top of the sauce. Cook, covered, for 10 to 15 minutes or until the fish flakes easily. Serve over the linguini. Makes 4 to 6 servings.

107

Entrées

Barbecued Shrimp

3 slices bacon, cooked, chopped
1 1/2 cups (3 sticks) butter, melted
2 tablespoons chopped yellow onion
2 garlic cloves, minced
2 tablespoons Dijon mustard
2 teaspoons cayenne pepper
1 tablespoon crab boil
1 1/2 teaspoons chili powder
1/2 teaspoon Tabasco sauce
1/2 teaspoon oregano
1/4 teaspoon basil
1/4 teaspoon thyme
1 1/2 pounds unpeeled shrimp

Combine the bacon, butter, onion, garlic, Dijon mustard, cayenne pepper, crab boil, chili powder, Tabasco sauce, oregano, basil and thyme in a bowl and mix well. Pour over the unpeeled shrimp in a large baking dish. Bake at 375 degrees for 20 minutes. Serve with a salad and crusty French bread to dip in the sauce. Makes 6 to 8 servings.

Note: *This is a great "hands-on" dish. Set the table with newspapers and pass out lots of paper napkins. Let everyone peel their own shrimp and toss the shells on the newspaper.*

Shrimp Scampi

1 pound peeled shrimp
1/2 cup (1 stick) butter
10 (or more) garlic cloves, pressed
1 tablespoon lemon juice
1/2 teaspoon oregano
1/8 teaspoon salt
1/8 teaspoon pepper
1/4 cup chopped fresh parsley

Place the shrimp in a single layer in a broiler pan. Heat the butter, garlic, lemon juice, oregano, salt and pepper in a saucepan over low heat until the butter is melted. Pour over the shrimp. Add the parsley and toss well, pressing the shrimp back into a single layer. Broil for 5 to 8 minutes or until the shrimp turn pink. Makes 4 servings.

Shrimp Roll-Ups for Two

2 slices bacon, cut into pieces
2 tablespoons chopped onion
2 medium tomatoes, chopped
Garlic powder and pepper to taste
8 peeled cooked jumbo shrimp
2 cups (8 ounces) shredded
Monterey Jack cheese
4 to 6 flour tortillas, heated
Chopped avocado and chopped cilantro

Cook the bacon in a large skillet until medium-crisp. Add the onion. Sauté until tender; drain. Add the tomatoes, garlic powder, pepper and shrimp. Cook for 1 to 2 minutes or until heated through. Stir in the cheese. Spoon into a greased 9×13-inch baking dish. Bake at 350 degrees for 3 to 5 minutes or until the cheese is melted. Spoon into the warm flour tortillas. Top with avocado and cilantro. Roll up the tortillas. Serve immediately. Makes 2 servings.

Luxurious Crab and Artichoke Casserole

3 tablespoons minced onion
1/2 cup (1 stick) butter
1/2 cup flour
4 cups cream (or 3 cups whole milk),
heated to boiling point
1/2 cup (or less) madeira
Salt and pepper to taste
4 cups (2 pounds) crab meat
2 tablespoons lemon juice
1 (8-ounce) can artichoke hearts,
drained, quartered
2 1/2 cups cooked shell pasta
1 (8-ounce) can button mushrooms
2 cups (8 ounces) shredded Gruyère cheese
Paprika to taste

Sauté the onion in the butter in a skillet until tender. Stir in the flour. Cook over medium heat for 2 minutes, stirring constantly. Remove from the heat. Whisk in the heated cream. Cook over medium heat until thickened, stirring constantly. Add the madeira, salt and pepper. Toss the crab meat with the lemon juice. Combine the cream sauce, crab meat, artichokes, pasta, mushrooms and 1 cup of the cheese in a buttered 6-quart casserole dish. Sprinkle with the remaining 1 cup cheese and paprika. Bake at 350 degrees for 25 to 30 minutes. Makes 10 to 12 servings.

Herbed Shrimp Casserole

2 eggs
1 cup evaporated milk
1 cup plain yogurt
8 ounces crumbled feta cheese
5 ounces shredded Swiss cheese
1/3 cup chopped fresh parsley
4 garlic cloves, minced
1 teaspoon each basil and oregano
8 ounces angel hair pasta, cooked
1 (15-ounce) can diced tomatoes
1 1/2 pounds medium shrimp, peeled
2 cups (8 ounces) shredded mozzarella cheese

Combine the eggs, evaporated milk, yogurt, feta cheese, Swiss cheese, parsley, garlic, basil and oregano in a bowl and mix well. Spread 1/2 of the pasta in an 8×12-inch baking dish coated with nonstick cooking spray. Drain the tomatoes partially and spoon 1/2 of the tomatoes evenly over the pasta. Top with 1/2 of the shrimp and the remaining pasta. Pour the egg mixture over the pasta and top with the remaining shrimp. Sprinkle the mozzarella cheese evenly over the top. Bake at 350 degrees for 30 minutes. Let stand for 10 minutes before serving. Makes 10 to 12 servings.

Tortellini Rafaella

2 cups chopped onions
4 garlic cloves, chopped
1/4 cup fresh basil
1/2 cup chopped fresh parsley
1 teaspoon cayenne pepper
1 tablespoon cracked black pepper
1/2 cup olive oil
4 pounds whole tomatoes, chopped
Salt to taste
2 (6-ounce) jars marinated artichoke hearts
2 (9-ounce) packages tortellini
1/4 cup (1 ounce) grated Romano cheese

Sauté the onions, garlic, basil, parsley, cayenne pepper and black pepper in the olive oil in a skillet for 5 minutes. Add the tomatoes and salt. Simmer, uncovered, over medium heat for 1 hour. Drain the artichokes, reserving the marinade; chop the artichokes. Add the artichoke marinade to the tomato mixture. Simmer for 30 minutes longer. Stir in the artichokes and simmer for 20 minutes or until the liquid is reduced to a thick sauce. Cook the tortellini using the package directions. Stir the tortellini and cheese into the tomato sauce. Serve hot or at room temperature. Makes 10 to 12 servings.

Linguini with Clam Sauce

1 garlic clove, finely chopped
1/4 cup (1/2 stick) butter or margarine
2 (6-ounce) cans chopped clams, liquid reserved
1/4 cup dry white wine
1/4 teaspoon cracked pepper
1 tablespoon chopped parsley
8 ounces linguini, cooked
Grated Parmesan cheese

Cook the garlic in the butter in a skillet until golden. Add the reserved clam liquid, wine and pepper. Simmer for 5 minutes, stirring occasionally. Add the clams and parsley. Cook until heated through. Serve over the linguini. Sprinkle with cheese. Makes 2 to 3 servings.

Red Clam Sauce

8 garlic cloves, minced
3 tablespoons vegetable oil
1 tablespoon butter
1 1/2 cups tomato sauce
2 teaspoons Worcestershire sauce
1 teaspoon sugar
1/2 teaspoon each dried basil, oregano and rosemary
1 (10-ounce) can whole baby clams, drained
Salt and pepper to taste
8 ounces pasta, cooked

Cook the garlic in the oil and butter in a skillet over low heat for 3 minutes or until the garlic begins to color. Add the tomato sauce, Worcestershire sauce, sugar, basil, oregano and rosemary and stir well. Simmer for 15 minutes or until thickened. Stir in the clams, salt and pepper. Simmer for 3 minutes longer. Serve over the pasta. Makes 2 to 3 servings.

Pasta Points

When serving pasta in large quantities, cook in small amounts. Remove from the heat and rinse immediately in cold water. Chill the pasta in cold water in the refrigerator until ready to serve. To heat, drop the pasta into boiling water for 1 minute; drain well.

Risotto con Porcini

1 small onion, finely chopped
2 tablespoons olive oil
2 tablespoons butter
1$^1/_2$ cups sliced porcini mushrooms or
other fresh mushrooms
2 cups arborio rice
6 cups hot chicken stock
Salt and freshly ground pepper to taste
$^1/_2$ cup (2 ounces) grated Parmesan cheese

Sauté the onion in the olive oil and butter in a large heavy saucepan over medium heat until the onion is tender. Add the mushrooms. Cook for 2 minutes, stirring constantly. Add the rice and stir to coat well with the oil and butter. Add the stock $^1/_2$ cup at a time. Cook for about 25 minutes, stirring constantly and allowing the rice to absorb most of the stock after each addition. Season with salt and pepper. Stir in the cheese or serve on the side. Makes 4 to 6 servings.

Quick Summertime Tomato and Shrimp Pasta

10 to 12 regular (or Roma) tomatoes, peeled,
cut into wedges or coarsely chopped
3 (or more) garlic cloves, chopped
$^1/_2$ cup (1 stick) butter or margarine
1 pound deveined peeled cooked large shrimp
$^1/_4$ to $^1/_2$ cup chopped fresh basil
Salt and pepper to taste
8 to 10 ounces spaghetti, fettuccini or
green spinach noodles, cooked
Freshly grated Parmesan cheese

Sauté the tomatoes and garlic in the butter in a large skillet for 5 minutes. Add the shrimp, basil, salt and pepper. Cook for 2 minutes or just until heated through. Serve over the pasta in bowls with cheese and French bread. Makes 4 to 5 servings.

Note: *Buy cooked cleaned shrimp from your neighborhood grocery store for a real time-saver.*

Shrimp in Tomato Feta Sauce

1/2 cup finely chopped onion

1 garlic clove, minced

6 tablespoons olive oil

1/2 cup dry white wine

3 (15-ounce) cans plum tomatoes, undrained, coarsely chopped

1 tablespoon finely chopped fresh parsley (preferably flat-leaf)

1/2 teaspoon basil

1/2 teaspoon oregano

3/4 teaspoon salt

Red pepper flakes to taste (optional)

1 1/2 pounds (about 34) medium shrimp, shelled, deveined

16 ounces rigatoni or other tubular pasta, cooked

8 ounces feta cheese, crumbled

Salt and pepper to taste

1 tablespoon finely chopped fresh parsley (preferably flat-leaf)

Cook the onion and garlic in the olive oil in a skillet over low heat until tender, stirring occasionally. Add the wine and boil for 1 minute. Stir in the tomatoes with their juice, 1 tablespoon parsley, basil, oregano, salt and red pepper flakes. Simmer for 5 minutes or until thickened, stirring occasionally. Add the shrimp. Cook over medium heat for 4 to 5 minutes or until the shrimp turn pink, stirring constantly. Stir in the pasta, 2/3 of the cheese, salt and pepper. Spoon into a greased 4-quart shallow baking dish. Sprinkle with parsley and the remaining cheese. Bake at 450 degrees for 20 minutes or until the cheese is bubbly and the top is crusty. Makes 6 servings.

Shrimp Sauté with Orzo

1 cup uncooked orzo or other tiny pasta
1 teaspoon olive oil
Salt and pepper to taste
2 garlic cloves, minced
1 tablespoon olive oil
20 deveined peeled shrimp with tails
2 tablespoons finely chopped flat-leaf parsley
Juice of 1 lemon
1 cup dry white wine
5 tablespoons unsalted butter
Zest of 1 lemon
1 tablespoon capers, rinsed
2 tablespoons finely chopped flat-leaf parsley

Cook the orzo using the package directions; drain. Toss the orzo with 1 teaspoon olive oil, salt and pepper.

Cook the garlic in 1 tablespoon olive oil in a large skillet for 1 minute. Add the shrimp, salt, pepper and 2 tablespoons parsley. Cook for 3 to 4 minutes on each side or until the shrimp turn pink. Remove the shrimp from the skillet and keep warm. Add the lemon juice and wine to the skillet. Bring to a boil. Reduce the heat and simmer for 2 minutes, stirring constantly. Remove from the heat. Stir in the butter, lemon zest, capers and 2 tablespoons parsley. Pour over the shrimp. Serve on the orzo. Makes 4 servings.

Mostaccioli with Spinach and Feta

8 ounces mostaccioli or penne pasta, cooked
2 tablespoons olive oil
3 cups chopped tomatoes
1 (10-ounce) package frozen chopped spinach, thawed, drained
1/2 cup chopped green onions
1 (8-ounce) package feta cheese with basil and tomato, crumbled

Combine the hot cooked pasta with the olive oil, tomatoes, spinach and green onions in a large saucepan. Cook for 2 minutes or until heated through, stirring constantly. Add the cheese. Cook for 1 minute longer. Makes 8 servings.

Note: *A handful of kalamata olives will add some flavor to this Greek-inspired pasta.*

Spinach Lasagna

1 cup chopped onion
1 cup sliced mushrooms
1 tablespoon vegetable oil
$1/3$ cup light cream cheese
$1/3$ cup sour cream
12 ounces cottage cheese
$1/2$ cup (2 ounces) grated Parmesan cheese
2 eggs
2 (10-ounce) packages frozen chopped
spinach, thawed, squeezed dry
Oven-ready lasagna noodles
1 (32-ounce) jar zesty mushroom
spaghetti sauce
1 cup (4 ounces) shredded mozzarella cheese
$1/2$ cup (2 ounces) grated Parmesan cheese
$1/2$ cup (2 ounces) shredded sharp
Cheddar cheese

Sauté the onion and mushrooms in the oil in a skillet until tender. Beat the cream cheese in a bowl until smooth. Add the sour cream, cottage cheese, $1/2$ cup Parmesan cheese and eggs and beat well. Combine the onion mixture, cream cheese mixture and spinach in a bowl and mix well. Layer $1/4$ of the spinach mixture, $1/2$ of the noodles, $1/4$ of the spinach mixture, $1/2$ of the spaghetti sauce, $1/2$ of the mozzarella cheese and $1/4$ cup of the Parmesan cheese in a greased 9×13-inch baking dish. Repeat the layers. Bake, covered, at 350 degrees for 50 minutes. Top with the Cheddar cheese. Bake, uncovered, for 10 minutes longer. Makes 10 to 12 servings.

115

Entrées

Grilled Vegetable Sandwiches

4 red bell peppers
4 large sweet onions, sliced
1 large eggplant, sliced into rounds
Olive oil
1/3 cup finely chopped thyme leaves
10 large 7-grain buns, split
Mayonnaise
2/3 cup chopped basil leaves
Salt and freshly ground pepper to taste

Grill the bell peppers over hot coals until tender and charred. Let stand until cool. Peel, seed and slice the bell peppers. Grill the onions and eggplant over hot coals for 3 to 5 minutes per side or until tender and charred, brushing with olive oil and sprinkling with the thyme during the grilling. Grill the buns cut side down, if desired. Spread both sides with mayonnaise. Layer the buns with the basil, grilled vegetables, salt and pepper. Makes 10 servings.

Caper Burgers

3 pounds ground chuck
20 to 25 capers, finely chopped
1 teaspoon ground black pepper
1 teaspoon garlic salt
1 teaspoon thyme
1 teaspoon oregano
1/4 teaspoon marjoram

Combine the ground chuck and capers in a bowl and mix well. Mix the pepper, garlic salt, thyme, oregano and marjoram together in a small bowl and add to the beef. Work the spices into the beef until well distributed. Shape the beef mixture into six 1/2-pound patties or twelve 1/4-pound patties. Grill over hot coals or broil on both sides to the desired degree of doneness. Serve on lightly toasted buns with lettuce, sliced tomatoes, red onion slices, mustard and ketchup. Makes 6 to 12 servings.

Fried Catfish Sandwiches with Curry Mayonnaise

¹/2 cup yellow cornmeal
¹/2 cup flour
¹/2 cup whole milk
4 (5-ounce) catfish fillets
Salt and pepper to taste
3 tablespoons olive oil
Curry Mayonnaise
1 (18-inch-long) French baguette,
cut crosswise into 4 pieces
1 large tomato, thinly sliced
4 Boston lettuce leaves

Combine the cornmeal and flour on a plate. Pour the milk into a shallow bowl. Dip each fillet into the milk; coat with the cornmeal mixture. Sprinkle with salt and pepper. Heat the olive oil in a large heavy skillet over medium-high heat. Cook the fillets in the hot oil for 5 minutes on each side or until cooked through and brown. Drain the fillets.

Cut each piece of bread in half horizontally. Spread the bottom halves with Curried Mayonnaise. Place the fillets on the bread bottoms. Top with the tomato, lettuce and bread tops. Makes 4 servings.

Curry Mayonnaise

¹/2 cup mayonnaise
1 tablespoon curry powder
1 tablespoon fresh lemon juice

Combine the mayonnaise, curry powder and lemon juice in a small bowl and mix well. Chill until serving time. Makes ¹/2 cup.

Chapter Recipes

Vegetables & Side Dishes

Roasted Asparagus

1 1/2 pounds asparagus
2 teaspoons olive oil
Salt and freshly ground pepper to taste
1 teaspoon balsamic vinegar

Snap off the tough ends of the asparagus and peel the stalks if desired. Toss the asparagus with the olive oil in a shallow roasting pan. Arrange in a single layer. Season with salt and pepper. Roast at 450 degrees for 10 to 15 minutes or until tender and brown, shaking once during the roasting. Sprinkle with the vinegar. Makes 4 servings.

Cheesy Lima Beans and Corn

1/2 cup (1 stick) butter or margarine
1 tablespoon flour
2 cups milk
4 ounces American cheese,
cut into small pieces
3 (10-ounce) boxes frozen baby lima beans
2 (10-ounce) boxes frozen corn
2 cups chopped green onion tops
1 small package potato chips,
broken into small pieces

Melt the butter in a skillet over medium-high heat. Whisk in the flour. Add the milk and cheese gradually. Cook until thickened and the cheese is melted, stirring constantly. Cook the lima beans and corn using the package directions; drain. Combine the lima beans, corn and green onions in a bowl. Add to the cheese sauce and mix lightly. Pour into a 9×13-inch ceramic baking dish. Sprinkle with the potato chips. Bake at 350 degrees for 30 minutes. Makes 8 to 10 servings.

Note: *You may prepare this casserole 2 or 3 days before serving. Let stand at room temperature for at least 30 minutes before baking. Allow 45 minutes for the baking time. This dish is good served alongside baked ham.*

Four-Bean Casserole

8 slices bacon, diced

1/2 cup chopped onion

1/2 cup ketchup

1/2 cup firmly packed brown sugar

1 1/2 tablespoons vinegar

1 tablespoon Worcestershire sauce

1/2 teaspoon salt

1 can lima beans, drained

1 can kidney beans, drained

1 large can green beans, undrained

Cook the bacon in a skillet until crisp. Remove the bacon; drain. Add the onion to the drippings in the skillet. Cook until tender. Combine the ketchup, brown sugar, vinegar, Worcestershire sauce and salt in a small bowl and mix well. Add with the beans to the skillet. Spoon into a greased casserole dish. Sprinkle with the bacon. Bake at 300 degrees for 45 to 60 minutes. Makes 12 servings.

Bundle of Beans

Fresh green beans
(10 or more for each bundle)

8 slices bacon

1/2 cup (1 stick) butter, melted

1 cup firmly packed brown sugar

2 tablespoons soy sauce

1/2 teaspoon garlic powder

Cook the green beans in boiling salted water just until tender; drain. Submerge the beans in ice water to stop the cooking process; drain. Dry the beans. Wrap 10 or more beans in a bundle with 1/2 a slice of bacon. Arrange the bundles in a baking dish. Mix the butter, brown sugar, soy sauce and garlic powder in a small bowl. Pour over the bean bundles. Marinate in the refrigerator for 3 to 4 hours or longer. Bake at 350 degrees for 25 minutes. Broil until the bacon is brown. Makes 8 servings.

Sesame Green Beans

1 pound green beans
1 teaspoon olive oil
2 teaspoons sesame seeds
Salt and freshly ground pepper to taste

Toss the green beans with the olive oil in a shallow roasting pan. Arrange in a single layer. Bake at 450 degrees for 12 minutes or until the beans are wrinkled, brown and tender, stirring once during the roasting. Toast the sesame seeds in a dry small skillet for 1 minute or until fragrant and light brown, stirring constantly. Crush the seeds lightly and toss with the beans. Season with salt and pepper. Makes 4 servings.

Note: *Asparagus is also delicious prepared this way.*

Governor's Sherried Green Beans

1/4 cup (1/2 stick) butter
1/4 cup light soy sauce
1/3 cup dry sherry (not cooking sherry)
2 pounds frozen green beans

Melt the butter in a large skillet over medium heat. Add the soy sauce, sherry and green beans and stir well. Cook, covered, over medium-low heat for 20 to 30 minutes or until tender, stirring occasionally. Add small amounts of water during the cooking if necessary. Makes 6 to 8 servings.

Corn Pudding

4 eggs, beaten
1 quart heavy cream
2 tablespoons sugar
1 teaspoon salt
6 (15-ounce) cans crispy niblet corn, drained
1 sleeve butter crackers, crushed
1/2 cup (1 stick) butter, melted

Beat the eggs with the cream, sugar and salt in a large bowl. Stir in the corn and 1/2 of the cracker crumbs. Pour into a greased 9×13-inch baking dish. Top with the remaining cracker crumbs and drizzle with the butter. Bake, uncovered, at 350 degrees for 1 hour. Makes 24 servings.

Corn Casserole

1 egg
1 package corn muffin mix
1 (15-ounce) can cream-style corn
1 (15-ounce) can whole kernel corn, drained
1 (4-ounce) can green chiles
1 cup sour cream
1/2 cup (1 stick) butter, melted
1/2 cup (2 ounces) shredded cheese

Mix the egg, corn muffin mix, corn, green chiles, sour cream and butter in a large bowl. Pour into a greased 3×9-inch casserole dish. Bake at 350 degrees for 30 minutes. Sprinkle with the cheese. Bake for 10 minutes longer. Makes 6 to 8 servings.

The Crucible Foundry

The Crucible Foundry is responsible for some of Oklahoma's most important pieces of art, including The Guardian, *which sits atop the state's capitol building. At the foundry, a variety of bronze sculptures are poured each day by artists from around the country. Visitors to the foundry, gallery, and sculpture garden can see all shapes and sizes of bronze artwork.*

Yukon Gold Potato and Arugula Gratin

2 1/2 cups heavy cream
1 1/2 cups whole milk
3 1/2 pounds Yukon Gold potatoes,
peeled, thinly sliced
Salt to taste
1 1/2 teaspoons freshly ground pepper
8 ounces arugula, coarsely chopped
2 cups (8 ounces) shredded Gruyère cheese
12 ounces bacon, crisp-cooked, crumbled

Combine the cream and milk in a 4-cup measuring cup and mix well. Layer 1/3 of the potatoes in a buttered 9×13-inch baking dish, overlapping the potatoes. Sprinkle with salt and some of the pepper. Layer 1/3 of the arugula, 1/3 of the cheese and 1/3 of the bacon over the potatoes. Pour 1 cup of the cream mixture over the top. Repeat the layers twice, topping with the remaining cream mixture. Bake at 375 degrees for 1 1/4 hours or until the potatoes are tender and the cream mixture has thickened. Let stand for 15 minutes before serving.
Makes 10 servings.

Scalloped Potatoes

1/4 cup (1/2 stick) butter
1/4 cup flour
2 cups milk
1 teaspoon salt or to taste
1/2 teaspoon pepper
1 cup (4 ounces) shredded sharp
Cheddar cheese
1/2 cup (2 ounces) grated Parmesan cheese
5 cups sliced peeled potatoes
1 small onion, chopped
Cracker crumbs

Melt the butter in a large saucepan. Whisk in the flour. Cook for 2 minutes over low heat, stirring constantly. Add the milk, salt and pepper. Cook until thickened, stirring constantly. Stir in the Cheddar cheese, Parmesan cheese, potatoes and onion. Pour into a greased 2-quart baking dish. Sprinkle with cracker crumbs. Bake, covered, at 350 degrees for 1 to 1 1/2 hours. Makes 4 to 6 servings.

Squash Casserole

1 package herb-seasoned stuffing mix
1 cup (2 sticks) butter, melted
2¹/2 pounds yellow squash, sliced
2 medium onions, sliced
1 teaspoon salt
1 (10-ounce) can cream of chicken soup
1 can water chestnuts, chopped
1 small jar pimento, chopped
1 cup sour cream
2 cups (8 ounces) shredded sharp
Cheddar cheese

Combine the stuffing mix and butter in a bowl and mix well. Spread ¹/2 of the stuffing mixture in a greased 9×13-inch baking dish. Cook the squash, onions and salt in boiling water to cover in a saucepan just until tender; drain. Combine the squash, onions, soup, water chestnuts, pimento and sour cream in a large bowl and mix well. Spread over the stuffing mixture. Top with the cheese and the remaining stuffing mixture. Bake at 350 degrees for 30 minutes. Makes 12 servings.

Note: *This casserole may be made ahead and frozen.*

Maple Squash and Sweet Potato Mash

1 (2¹/2-pound) butternut squash, peeled,
seeded, cut into chunks
4 (8-ounce) sweet potatoes, peeled,
cut into chunks
¹/4 cup Vermont maple syrup
2 tablespoons unsalted butter
¹/2 teaspoon nutmeg
Salt and freshly ground pepper to taste

Bring the squash and sweet potatoes to a boil in salted water to cover in a saucepan. Reduce the heat and simmer for 15 to 20 minutes or until tender; drain. Add the maple syrup, butter, nutmeg, salt and pepper and mash with a fork. Spoon into a greased baking dish. Bake, covered, at 350 degrees just until heated through. Makes 8 servings.

Note: *A handful of chopped toasted or sugared pecans sprinkled over the top of this dish adds flavor and crunch as well as eye appeal.*

Mrs. Wilkes' Boardinghouse Sweet Potato Soufflé

4 pounds sweet potatoes, peeled, sliced
1 1/2 cups sugar
1/2 cup (1 stick) butter or margarine
1/2 cup evaporated milk
1/2 cup raisins
2 eggs
1/2 cup chopped pecans
1/2 cup shredded coconut
1/2 teaspoon nutmeg
Juice and grated zest of 1 lemon
Miniature marshmallows

Boil the sweet potatoes in salted water to cover in a saucepan until tender; drain. Mash the potatoes. Add the sugar, butter, evaporated milk, raisins, eggs, pecans, coconut, nutmeg, lemon juice and lemon zest in a large bowl and mix well. Spoon into a greased baking dish. Bake at 350 degrees for 30 minutes, topping with a layer of marshmallows during the last few minutes of baking. Makes 8 servings.

Italian Zucchini

2 pounds zucchini, sliced
1 pound mushrooms, sliced
1 bunch green onions, chopped
2 tablespoons extra-virgin olive oil
1 (8-ounce) can tomato sauce
3 garlic cloves, minced
3 tablespoons extra-virgin olive oil
Dash of basil
1/2 cup red wine (optional)
8 ounces sliced Monterey Jack cheese
6 tablespoons grated Parmesan cheese

Sauté the zucchini, mushrooms and green onions in 2 tablespoons olive oil in a skillet until the zucchini is tender. Combine the tomato sauce, garlic, 3 tablespoons olive oil, basil and wine in a saucepan. Simmer over low heat for 2 to 3 minutes. Layer the zucchini mixture, tomato sauce mixture and Monterey Jack cheese in a lightly greased 2-quart baking dish. Top with the Parmesan cheese. Bake at 350 degrees for 30 to 40 minutes or until bubbly. Makes 8 to 10 servings.

Lemon Rice Pilaf

4 ribs celery, sliced
6 green onions, chopped
2 tablespoons plus 1 teaspoon butter, melted
3 cups cooked rice
2 tablespoons grated lemon zest
1/2 teaspoon salt
1/4 teaspoon pepper
Lemon slices

Sauté the celery and green onions in the butter in a large skillet over medium heat until the celery is tender. Add the rice, lemon zest, salt and pepper. Cook over low heat for 2 minutes or until heated through, stirring constantly. Garnish with lemon slices. Makes 6 servings.

Note: *This is an excellent side dish with Asian foods.*

Oyster Dressing

3 pints raw oysters
1 loaf stale French bread, broken into pieces
1 bunch green onions, chopped
1 medium onion, chopped
3 or 4 garlic cloves, chopped
1 tablespoon butter or margarine
2 eggs
2 tablespoons chopped fresh parsley
Fresh thyme leaves
Salt and pepper to taste
2 tablespoons butter or margarine, melted

Cook the oysters in their liquid in an iron skillet over medium heat until the edges curl; drain, reserving the liquid. Soak the bread in the oyster liquid. Combine the bread and oysters in a wooden bowl. Chop the bread and oysters into very small pieces.

Sauté the green onions, onion and garlic in 1 tablespoon butter in the skillet until tender. Add the oyster mixture, eggs, parsley, thyme leaves, salt and pepper and mix well. Stir in 2 tablespoons butter. Heat for 10 minutes, stirring constantly. Bake at 350 degrees for 30 minutes or use to stuff a 10- to 12-pound turkey. Makes 8 servings.

127

Vegetables & Side Dishes

Chapter Recipes

Tailgates & Parties

Avocado Dip

4 cups (1 pound) shredded
Monterey Jack cheese
3 tomatoes, chopped
1/2 cup zesty Italian dressing
1 (6-ounce) can green chiles, chopped
2 avocados, chopped

Combine the cheese, tomatoes, Italian dressing and green chiles in a bowl and mix well. Chill until serving time. Add the avocados and mix well. Serve with tortilla chips. Makes 40 to 50 servings.

Sugared Bacon

1 pound bacon
1 1/4 cups firmly packed brown sugar
1 tablespoon cinnamon

Cut each bacon slice in half. Combine the brown sugar and cinnamon in a bowl and mix well. Coat each 1/2 slice of bacon with the brown sugar mixture. Twist the slices and arrange them on a rack in a broiler pan. Bake at 350 degrees for 15 to 20 minutes or until the bacon is crisp and the sugar is bubbly. Cool on a sheet of foil. Serve at room temperature. Makes 25 to 30 servings.

Avocado Advice

To test an avocado for ripeness, try to flick off the small stem. If it comes off easily and there is green underneath, the avocado is ripe. If the stem does not come off or if there is brown underneath the stem after prying it off, the avocado is not yet useable.

Savory Cream Cheese Ball

1 (8-ounce) tub onion and chives
cream cheese, softened
1 (8-ounce) package cream cheese, softened
1 cup (4 ounces) shredded Cheddar cheese
3 fresh chives, chopped
1 package ranch salad dressing mix
Chopped pecans

Combine the cream cheeses, Cheddar cheese, chives and salad dressing mix in a bowl and mix well. Shape into a ball and roll in chopped pecans. Serve with crackers. Makes 8 to 10 servings.

Chicken Pillows

2 (3-ounce) packages cream cheese
with chives, softened
$1^1/4$ cups ($2^1/2$ sticks) butter, softened
$1/8$ teaspoon pepper
2 cups chopped cooked chicken
1 (4-ounce) can mushrooms, drained
2 (8-count) cans crescent rolls
1 cup (2 sticks) butter, melted
$1/2$ cup finely chopped walnuts
2 cups herb-flavored stuffing mix,
finely crushed

Beat the cream cheese, softened butter and pepper in a bowl until smooth. Fold in the chicken and mushrooms. Unroll the crescent roll dough and separate the rolls. Spread the chicken filling over each roll. Roll up from the wide ends; seal the edges to enclose the filling. Dip each roll in the melted butter; coat with the walnuts, then the crushed stuffing mix. Place the rolls on an ungreased baking sheet. Bake at 325 degrees for 20 to 30 minutes. Makes 16 servings.

Note: *These rolls may be prepared and then frozen before they are baked. Defrost slightly and bake as above.*

Spanakopita

1 large onion, chopped
2 tablespoons minced garlic
1 bunch green onions, chopped
¹/4 cup olive oil
2 (10-ounce) packages frozen chopped
spinach, cooked, squeezed dry
¹/4 cup dried or chopped fresh parsley
2 tablespoons dill weed
¹/2 teaspoon salt
¹/2 teaspoon pepper
1 pound traditional feta cheese, crumbled
4 eggs, beaten
Butter-flavor nonstick cooking spray
1 box phyllo dough

Cook the onion, garlic and green onions in the olive oil in a skillet over medium heat for 5 minutes, stirring frequently. Add the spinach. Cook for 5 minutes longer. Stir in the parsley, dill weed, salt and pepper. Cook until the liquid evaporates and the spinach begins to stick, stirring constantly. Let cool to room temperature. Stir in the cheese and beat in the eggs 1 at a time. Chill for up to 24 hours.

Coat a 9×13-inch baking dish with cooking spray. Lay 1 sheet of the phyllo dough in the dish, pressing into the corners and against the sides. Spray the dough with cooking spray. Continue to layer and spray the phyllo sheets for a total of 10 sheets, or ¹/2 of the package. Spoon the spinach mixture evenly over the dough. Place 1 sheet of dough over the spinach. Continue spraying and layering the remaining sheets. Trim excess dough. Spray the top layer with cooking spray. Bake at 300 degrees for 1 hour. Cut into squares. Makes 12 servings.

Working with Phyllo Dough

Delicate phyllo dough is easier to handle when kept moist. Start by unrolling the paper-thin sheets of dough and topping with waxed paper and then a damp kitchen towel (if the damp towel touches the dough directly, it will become gooey). Keep the towel in place as you work; pull aside to peel off layers of dough. Phyllo tears very easily, so work carefully. Keep any scraps or trimmings to use later when patching. Brush very lightly with melted butter; do not saturate the paper-thin dough, or it will come out greasy.

Puff Pastry Pouch

The savory filling
$1/2$ cup chopped mushrooms
$1/4$ cup chopped green onions
$1/4$ cup chopped black olives
Salt and freshly ground pepper to taste
1 wedge Brie cheese

For the savory filling, combine the mushrooms, green onions, olives, salt and pepper in a bowl and mix well. Remove the rind from the Brie and divide the cheese into small pieces.

The sweet filling
$1/2$ cup raspberry jam
$1/2$ cup chopped walnuts
1 wedge Gouda cheese

For the sweet filling, combine the raspberry jam and walnuts in a small bowl and mix well. Slice the Gouda into $1/4$-inch slices.

The pouch
1 roll frozen puff pastry

For the pouch, unfold the puff pastry using the package directions and roll slightly to form a square shape. Spoon $1/2$ of either filling over the center of the pastry. Cover with the Brie or Gouda cheese. Spoon the remaining $1/2$ of the filling over the cheese. Bring the edges of the pastry up over the filling to form a pouch. Tie gently with cooking string. Spray the pastry with nonstick cooking spray. Bake at 400 degrees for 11 to 13 minutes or until golden brown. Remove the string and tie carefully with a decorative ribbon before serving. Place a knife beside the pouch for guests to cut off individual servings. Makes 10 to 12 servings.

Note: *You may also use phyllo dough to make the pouch.*

Apricot Pecans

¹/2 cup apricot nectar
1¹/2 cups sugar
2 teaspoons grated lemon zest
1 teaspoon butter
2¹/2 cups pecan halves

Combine the apricot nectar and sugar in a 2-quart saucepan and mix well. Cook, uncovered, over medium heat to 234 to 240 degrees on a candy thermometer, soft-ball stage. Remove from the heat. Stir in the lemon zest and butter. Add the pecans. Beat until the mixture thickens and loses its luster. Pour onto waxed paper and let stand until cool. Break into serving-size pieces. Makes 15 to 20 servings.

Spiced Apple Cider

¹/2 gallon apple cider
1 cup sugar
2 teaspoons whole cloves
1 whole nutmeg
2 cups orange juice
¹/2 cup apple brandy (optional)
Cinnamon sticks

Combine the apple cider and sugar in a Dutch oven. Tie the cloves and nutmeg in a cheesecloth bag and add to the cider mixture. Bring to a boil. Reduce the heat and simmer for 15 minutes. Discard the spice bag. Stir in the orange juice and apple brandy. Cook just until heated through. Serve in mugs with cinnamon sticks. Makes 10 to 12 servings.

Twelve-Hour Pork Roast with Lemon Pan Sauce

1 whole (7- to 9-pound) pork shoulder
12 garlic cloves, finely chopped
1 (2-ounce) bottle fennel seeds
Salt and freshly ground pepper to taste
8 small dried red chiles, crumbled
Juice of 6 lemons
4 tablespoons olive oil
Lemon Pan Sauce

Score the pork shoulder at $1/4$-inch intervals, cutting deeply into the pork. Combine the garlic, fennel seeds, salt, pepper and red chiles in a food processor and pulse until coarsely ground. Rub the spice mixture into the pork shoulder, pressing it into the skin and cut areas. Place the shoulder on a rack in a roasting pan. Roast at 450 degrees for 30 minutes or until the skin begins to crackle and brown. Loosen the shoulder from the pan bottom and pour $1/2$ of the juice of 6 lemons and 2 tablespoons of the olive oil over the roast. Reduce the oven temperature to 250 degrees. Roast for 12 to 18 hours or until the skin is crispy and the pork is falling from the bone, basting with the remaining juice of 6 lemons and olive oil during the cooking. Remove the pork to a serving platter. Spoon the Lemon Pan Sauce over the roast pork. Serve some of the crisp skin along with the meat. Makes 10 to 12 servings.

Lemon Pan Sauce

3 tablespoons pan drippings
1 (14-ounce) can chicken broth
Juice of 2 lemons

Drain all but 3 tablespoons of the fat from the roasting pan. Heat the drippings over medium heat, scraping up the browned bits on the bottom of the pan. Add the chicken broth and juice of 2 lemons. Simmer, continuing to scrape the bottom of the pan, for 5 minutes or until reduced.

Pork Tenderloin with Plum Sauce

1 pork tenderloin
1/2 cup teriyaki sauce
1/2 cup soy sauce
3 tablespoons firmly packed brown sugar
3 tablespoons vegetable oil
Onion flakes
1/2 teaspoon ginger
1/2 teaspoon dry mustard
Plum Sauce

Place the pork tenderloin in a shallow baking dish. Whisk the teriyaki sauce, soy sauce, brown sugar, oil, onion flakes, ginger and dry mustard together in a bowl and pour over the tenderloin. Marinate in the refrigerator for 4 hours or longer. Grill the meat over hot coals until done. Slice into medallions and spoon Plum Sauce over each serving. Makes 4 to 6 servings.

Plum Sauce

1/4 cup plum preserves
1/4 cup whole cranberry sauce
3 tablespoons sherry
1 teaspoon soy sauce

Combine the plum preserves, cranberry sauce, sherry and soy sauce in a small saucepan. Cook over medium-high heat for 5 to 10 minutes. Makes 2/3 cup.

Marinated Brisket

1 (8- to 10-pound) brisket, well trimmed
1 1/2 tablespoons salt
1 1/2 tablespoons paprika
1 teaspoon garlic powder
1 package onion soup mix

Place the brisket on a large sheet of heavy-duty foil. Combine the salt, paprika, garlic powder and a little water to moisten in a small bowl and mix well. Rub the mixture on both sides of the brisket. Sprinkle the onion soup mix over the top. Seal the foil around the roast. Bake at 425 degrees for 1 hour. Reduce the temperature to 375 degrees. Bake for 2 hours longer. Reduce the temperature to 325 degrees. Bake for 1 hour or until the brisket is fork-tender. Makes 12 to 16 servings.

Note: *This brisket is delicious hot from the oven, and the leftovers make great sandwiches.*

Tailgate Beef Sandwiches

1 (4-pound) chuck or rump roast
1 tablespoon garlic salt
1/2 tablespoon oregano
1/4 tablespoon rosemary
3/4 tablespoon seasoned salt
2 beef bouillon cubes
Dash of crushed red pepper
Freshly ground black pepper to taste

Combine the roast and water to barely cover in a Dutch oven. Add the remaining ingredients. Bake, covered, at 250 degrees for 8 hours or until fork-tender. Shred the roast and serve on buttered toasted buns or French rolls. Serve the pan drippings in small bowls for dipping. Makes 10 to 12 servings.

Note: *Try cooking this roast overnight or in a slow cooker. It's a great crowd pleaser and men, especially, love these sandwiches.*

Picadillo

2 pounds ground beef
1 cup chopped onion
2/3 cup green bell pepper, chopped
1 (16-ounce) can diced tomatoes, undrained
1/4 cup Worcestershire sauce
2 teaspoons minced garlic
2 1/4 teaspoons salt
1/4 teaspoon each cayenne and black pepper
1/2 teaspoon each cumin and oregano
2 cans concentrated beef broth
2 (6-ounce) cans tomato paste
1 (4-ounce) jar chopped pimentos
1 or 2 (4-ounce) cans chopped black olives
1 (4-ounce) can chopped green chiles
1 (6-ounce) can mushroom stems and pieces
1 cup each slivered almonds and dark raisins

Brown the beef in a skillet until crumbly; drain. Stir in the onion, bell pepper, tomatoes, Worcestershire sauce, garlic, salt, cayenne pepper, black pepper, cumin and oregano. Cook over medium heat until the vegetables are tender. Add the broth, tomato paste, pimentos, olives, green chiles, mushrooms, almonds and raisins. Simmer for 1 hour, stirring occasionally. Serve with corn chips or tortillas or over rice. Makes 20 hors d'oeuvre servings, or 8 entrée servings.

Warms-You-to-the-Bone Chili

2 pounds lean ground beef
1 pound bulk pork sausage
1 medium onion, cut into 1/4-inch pieces
3 packages chili seasoning
2 (15-ounce) cans whole tomatoes, chopped
1 to 2 tablespoons chopped jalapeño chiles
1 (15-ounce) can kidney beans or navy beans
1 (15-ounce) can hominy
Shredded Cheddar cheese

Brown the beef, sausage and onion in a skillet until the beef and sausage are crumbly; drain. Add the chili seasoning, 2 to 3 cups water, tomatoes, jalapeño chiles, kidney beans and hominy. Bring to a boil. Reduce the heat and simmer for 30 to 60 minutes. Top each serving with Cheddar cheese. Makes 8 to 10 servings.

White Chicken Tetrazzini

2 chickens
1 onion, quartered
1 bay leaf
1 cup mushrooms, thinly sliced
1 cup (2 sticks) butter
1 bunch green onions, thinly sliced
4 cups half-and-half
3 tablespoons dry sherry
1/4 cup white wine
2 tablespoons parsley
2 (2-ounce) jars chopped pimento
3 teaspoons salt
1/4 teaspoon cayenne pepper
1/2 teaspoon black pepper
1/4 cup (1/2 stick) butter, melted
1/4 cup flour
2 (4-ounce) cans sliced water chestnuts
15 ounces linguini
1 (16-ounce) package frozen peas
1 cup (4 ounces) freshly grated
Parmesan cheese

Combine the chickens, onion, bay leaf and salted water to cover in a large stockpot. Bring to a boil. Reduce the heat and simmer for 45 to 60 minutes. Remove the chicken and let stand until cool. Strain and reserve the broth, discarding the solids. Chop the chicken, discarding the skin and bones.

Sauté the mushrooms in 1 cup butter in a skillet for 3 to 5 minutes. Add the green onions, half-and-half, sherry, wine, parsley, pimento, salt, cayenne pepper and black pepper. Cook until heated through. Blend 1/4 cup butter and the flour to a paste consistency in a small bowl. Stir into the mushroom mixture with the chicken and water chestnuts. Cook until smooth and thickened, stirring constantly.

Bring the reserved chicken broth to a boil in a large stockpot and stir in the linguini. Cook until tender, adding more water if necessary; drain. Stir the pasta and frozen peas into the chicken mixture. Spoon into 2 greased 9×13-inch baking dishes. Top with the cheese. Bake at 375 degrees for 20 minutes or until heated through. Makes 16 to 20 servings.

Note: *To make this recipe less time-consuming, cook and chop the chicken the day before.*

Chicken and Spinach Casserole

3 pounds chicken breasts

5 ounces fine egg noodles

1/4 cup (1/2 stick) butter

1/4 cup flour

1 cup milk

2 cups sour cream

1/3 cup lemon juice

1 teaspoon salt

2 teaspoons seasoned salt

2 teaspoons black pepper

1/4 teaspoon cayenne pepper

2 (10-ounce) packages frozen chopped spinach, cooked, drained

8 ounces mushrooms, sliced

1 (8-ounce) can sliced water chestnuts

1 (2-ounce) jar pimentos, drained

1/2 cup chopped onion

1/2 cup chopped celery

Toasted almonds (optional)

1 1/2 cups (6 ounces) shredded Cheddar cheese

Cook the chicken in salted water to cover in a stockpot until tender. Let stand until cool. Chop the chicken, discarding the skin and bones. Reserve the stock. Cook the noodles using the package directions; drain.

Melt the butter in a saucepan and whisk in the flour. Add the milk and 1 cup of the reserved chicken stock. Cook over low heat until thickened, stirring constantly. Add the sour cream, lemon juice, salt, seasoned salt, black pepper and cayenne pepper and mix well. Fold in the noodles, spinach, mushrooms, water chestnuts, pimento, onion, celery and almonds. Spoon 1/2 of the spinach mixture into a buttered 3-quart casserole dish. Top with 1/2 of the chicken. Repeat with the remaining spinach mixture and chicken. Top with the cheese. Bake, uncovered, at 350 degrees for 25 to 30 minutes. Makes 12 to 14 servings.

Note: *You may prepare this casserole a day or two ahead and chill until time to bake. Do not freeze it.*

Lime-Marinated Salmon with Ginger Lime Butter

2 cups coarsely chopped onions
2 large jalapeño chiles, seeded, minced
$1/3$ cup fresh lime juice
$1/4$ cup olive oil
1 bunch fresh cilantro, coarsely chopped
$1^{1}/2$ teaspoons coarsely chopped garlic
1 tablespoon honey
(or chile honey if available)
1 teaspoon salt
2 pounds salmon fillets, cut into
4- to 5-ounce portions
Salt and pepper to taste
Ginger Lime Butter

Combine the onions, jalapeño chiles, lime juice, olive oil, cilantro, garlic, honey and 1 teaspoon salt in a food processor and pulse for 30 seconds. Taste the marinade and adjust the seasonings. Pour $1/2$ of the marinade in a glass or stainless steel baking dish. Place the salmon fillets in the dish and cover with the remaining marinade. Let stand at room temperature for 1 to 3 hours. Wipe the marinade from the salmon and sprinkle with salt and pepper to taste. Grill over hot coals to the desired degree of doneness. Top each portion with Ginger Lime Butter. Makes 6 to 8 servings.

Ginger Lime Butter

$1/2$ cup (1 stick) butter, softened
1 tablespoon freshly grated gingerroot
$1/3$ cup coarsely chopped fresh cilantro
$1^{1}/2$ teaspoons fresh lime juice
$1/2$ teaspoon salt

Combine the butter, gingerroot, cilantro, lime juice and salt in a food processor and pulse until smooth. Store in the refrigerator if not using within 45 minutes. Makes 6 to 8 servings.

Sweet-and-Sour Grilled Salmon

3 tablespoons Dijon mustard
3 tablespoons low-sodium soy sauce
3 tablespoons firmly packed dark brown sugar
3 tablespoons safflower oil
1 teaspoon prepared horseradish
4 (8-ounce) salmon steaks

Combine the Dijon mustard, soy sauce, brown sugar, safflower oil and horseradish in a small bowl and mix well. Brush the salmon steaks with 1/2 of the mixture. Marinate, covered, in the refrigerator for up to 6 hours. Grill over hot coals for 5 minutes. Turn the steaks and brush with the remaining marinade. Grill until the fish flakes easily. Serve hot or at room temperature with rice and a salad. Makes 4 servings.

Note: *Other nice accompaniments to this salmon are tiny fresh asparagus and a squash soufflé.*

Asparagus Salad

1 pound asparagus spears, trimmed
(peeled if desired)
1/4 cup white balsamic vinegar
2 teaspoons prepared horseradish
2 teaspoons Dijon mustard
2 teaspoons honey
2 teaspoons paprika
1 teaspoon garlic powder
1/2 teaspoon olive oil
1/2 teaspoon pepper
Diced tomatoes
Crumbled blue cheese

Cook the asparagus in boiling salted water in a skillet until tender-crisp; drain. Combine the vinegar, horseradish, Dijon mustard, honey, paprika, garlic powder, olive oil and pepper in a jar and shake well. Pour the dressing over the asparagus in a serving bowl. Garnish with diced tomatoes and cheese. Makes 4 to 6 servings.

Black Bean Salad

2 cans black beans, drained, rinsed
3 ears of corn, cooked, kernels cut from cobs
2 large tomatoes, peeled, seeded, chopped
1 avocado, chopped
1 small red onion, chopped
1/3 cup chopped fresh cilantro
2 fresh jalapeño chiles, seeded, minced
2 tablespoons extra-virgin olive oil
1 tablespoon red wine vinegar
1/4 cup fresh lime juice
1 teaspoon salt
1/2 teaspoon freshly ground pepper

Combine the black beans, corn kernels, tomatoes, avocado, onion, cilantro and jalapeño chiles in a salad bowl. Combine the olive oil, vinegar, lime juice, salt and pepper in a jar and shake well. Pour the dressing over the salad and toss gently. Makes 8 servings.

Note: *This salad can be made ahead and is delicious with any southwestern menu.*

Black-Eyed Peas

1 pound dried black-eyed peas
1 large can diced tomatoes
2 onions, quartered
1 rib celery, cut in several pieces
6 garlic cloves
2 teaspoons chopped fresh parsley
Chicken broth (optional)
1 pound Italian sausage, sliced into small pieces
3 bay leaves
1 teaspoon thyme
Salt and pepper to taste
1/2 cup red wine

Soak the peas in water to cover in a large saucepan for 8 to 10 hours; drain. Combine the tomatoes, onions, celery, garlic and parsley in a food processor and pulse until the vegetables are pea-size. Add to the drained peas in the saucepan. Add water and/or chicken broth to cover, sausage, bay leaves, thyme, salt and pepper. Bring to a boil. Reduce the heat and simmer for 2 to 3 hours or until the peas are tender. Discard the bay leaves. Add the wine just before serving. Makes 8 to 10 servings.

Vermicelli Pasta Salad

12 ounces vermicelli, broken into small pieces
1 tablespoon MSG
1 tablespoon seasoned salt
3 tablespoons lemon juice
2 cups finely chopped celery
1 cup finely chopped onion
1 cup finely chopped green bell pepper
1 (4-ounce) jar diced pimentos, undrained
1 (4-ounce) can chopped black olives
1 (8-ounce) can water chestnuts,
chopped, rinsed
1 cup mayonnaise

Cook the vermicelli using the package directions; drain. Combine the vermicelli, MSG, seasoned salt and lemon juice in a salad bowl. Chill for 8 to 10 hours. Stir in the celery, onion, bell pepper, pimento, olives, water chestnuts and mayonnaise and mix well. Makes 10 to 12 servings.

Tailgates & Parties

Boyd House

Built in 1906 as the private residence of David Ross Boyd, the house became the official residence of University of Oklahoma presidents in 1914. Between 1914 and 1922, the house was remodeled to fit the new attitude of the university. The house is significant in that it represents a shift in the university's image from that of a mediocre school to that of a respected university of academic quality. The Neoclassical Revival style reflected a sense of tradition, permanence, and classical learning. From its corner site overlooking the University of Oklahoma campus, it has housed the presidents of the state's primary institute of higher learning.

Shoe Peg Corn Bake

1/4 cup (1/2 stick) butter or margarine
1 (8-ounce) package cream cheese
1/4 cup milk
3 cans Shoe Peg corn, drained
1 (4-ounce) can diced green chiles
1/2 teaspoon garlic salt
1/2 teaspoon pepper
1 cup (4 ounces) shredded American or
Cheddar cheese

Heat the butter, cream cheese and milk in a saucepan over low heat until smooth, stirring constantly. Add the corn, green chiles, garlic salt and pepper. Spoon into a greased baking dish and top with the cheese. Bake at 350 degrees for 25 minutes. Makes 12 to 16 servings.

Garlic Cheese Grits

1 cup instant grits
4 cups water
1 teaspoon salt
1 roll garlic cheese, cut in pieces
1/2 cup (1 stick) butter, cut in pieces
1 egg, beaten
1 teaspoon Worcestershire sauce
1/2 teaspoon Tabasco sauce
1 teaspoon pepper
Parsley flakes

Cook the grits, water and salt in a saucepan using the package directions. Remove from the heat. Add the garlic cheese, butter, egg, Worcestershire sauce, Tabasco sauce and pepper and stir until smooth. Pour into a buttered baking dish and sprinkle with parsley flakes. Bake, uncovered, at 300 degrees for 1 hour. Makes 12 to 16 servings.

Note: *This dish freezes well.*

Sausage Bread

2 (1-pound) loaves frozen
white bread dough, thawed
1 pound bulk pork sausage
1 1/2 cups sliced mushrooms
1/2 cup chopped onion
2 eggs
2 1/2 cups (10 ounces) shredded
mozzarella cheese
1 teaspoon each basil, parsley flakes, crushed
rosemary and garlic powder
1 egg, beaten

Let the dough rise, covered, in a warm place until doubled in bulk. Cook the sausage in a skillet until crumbly. Add the mushrooms and onion. Sauté until the vegetables are tender; drain. Let stand until cool. Mix in the next 6 ingredients. Roll each dough portion into a 12×16-inch rectangle. Spread 1/2 of the sausage mixture over each rectangle, leaving a 1-inch edge. Roll as for a jelly roll from the short side and seal the edges. Place seam side down on a greased baking sheet. Bake at 350 degrees for 25 minutes. Brush with 1 egg. Bake for 5 to 10 minutes or until golden brown. Makes 2 loaves.

Pineapple Zucchini Bread

3 eggs
2 cups sugar
1 cup vegetable oil
2 teaspoons vanilla
2 cups coarsely grated zucchini
1 (8-ounce) can crushed pineapple, drained
3 cups flour
2 teaspoons baking soda
1 teaspoon salt
1/2 teaspoon baking powder
1 1/2 teaspoons cinnamon
3/4 teaspoon nutmeg
1 cup each raisins and chopped nuts

Combine the eggs, sugar, oil and vanilla in a mixing bowl and beat until thick and foamy. Stir in the zucchini and pineapple. Mix the flour, baking soda, salt, cinnamon and nutmeg in a bowl. Stir in the raisins and nuts. Add to the zucchini mixture, stirring just until mixed. Spoon into 2 greased and floured loaf pans. Bake at 350 degrees for 1 hour or until the loaves test done. Cool in the pans for 10 minutes. Remove to a wire rack to cool completely. Makes 2 loaves.

Banana Nut Cake

3/4 cup (1 1/2 sticks) butter, softened
1 1/2 cups mashed bananas (3 or 4)
2 cups sugar
3/4 cup whole milk
3 cups flour
1 1/2 teaspoons baking powder
1 1/2 teaspoons baking soda
1 teaspoon salt
2 eggs
2 teaspoons vanilla extract
1 1/2 cups chopped pecans or walnuts
Confectioners' sugar to taste

Cream the butter with the bananas in a mixing bowl. Add the sugar and milk and beat until light and fluffy. Combine the next 4 ingredients in a small bowl. Add to the banana mixture a little at a time, beating well after each addition. Beat in the eggs and vanilla. Stir in the pecans. Pour into a greased and floured bundt pan. Bake at 350 degrees for 50 to 60 minutes or until the cake tests done. Cool in the pan for 15 minutes. Invert onto a serving plate and cool completely. Sift confectioners' sugar over the cake. Makes 8 to 12 servings.

Sour Cream Chocolate Chip Cake

6 tablespoons butter, softened
1 cup sugar
2 eggs
1 1/3 cups flour
1 1/2 teaspoons baking powder
1 teaspoon baking soda
1 teaspoon cinnamon
1 cup sour cream
1 cup (6 ounces) semisweet chocolate chips
1 tablespoon sugar

Cream the butter and 1 cup sugar in a bowl until light and fluffy. Beat in the eggs 1 at a time. Sift the flour, baking powder, baking soda and cinnamon together. Add to the creamed mixture and blend well. Stir in the sour cream. Pour into a greased and floured 9×13-inch cake pan. Sprinkle the chocolate chips over the batter. Sprinkle 1 tablespoon sugar over the top. Bake at 350 degrees for 35 minutes or until the cake pulls away from the sides of the pan. Serve the cake warm or cool with a dollop of whipped cream, if desired. Makes 12 servings.

Blondie Swirl Bars

1/2 cup (1 stick) butter or margarine
1 1/2 cup firmly packed light brown sugar
2 eggs
1 teaspoon vanilla extract
1 1/2 cups flour
2 teaspoons baking powder
1/2 teaspoon salt
1/2 cup chopped pecans
1 cup (6 ounces) semisweet chocolate chips

Melt the butter in a large saucepan. Add the brown sugar and stir over low heat until well combined. Let stand until cool. Beat in the eggs 1 at a time. Stir in the vanilla. Stir in a mixture of the flour, baking powder and salt. Fold in the pecans and 1/4 cup of the chocolate chips. Spread the batter in a greased and floured 9×13-inch baking pan. Sprinkle with the remaining chocolate chips. Bake at 350 degrees for 3 minutes. Remove from the oven and swirl the batter with a knife. Bake for 20 minutes longer. Cool in the pan. Cut into bars. Makes 24 servings.

Sticky Pecan Pie Bars

1 package plain yellow cake mix
1/2 cup (1 stick) butter, melted
1 egg
3/4 cup dark corn syrup
1/4 cup firmly packed light brown sugar
2 eggs
1 teaspoon vanilla extract
1 1/2 cups chopped pecans

Beat the cake mix, butter and 1 egg in a mixing bowl at low speed for 2 minutes or until a thick dough forms. Press over the bottom and 1/2 inch up the sides of a greased 9×13-inch baking pan, using the fingers to spread and smooth the dough. Bake at 350 degrees for 20 minutes or until brown. Beat the corn syrup, brown sugar, 2 eggs and vanilla in the same mixing bowl at medium speed for 1 minute. Fold in the pecans. Spread over the crust. Bake at 350 degrees for 22 to 25 minutes or until golden brown and the filling is just beginning to set. Cool on a wire rack for 30 minutes. Cut into bars. Makes 24 servings.

Cherry Nut Bonbons

6 tablespoons butter, melted
2 tablespoons heavy cream
16 ounces dry fondant powder
(available at cake and candy supply stores)
1 (10-ounce) jar maraschino cherries,
drained, chopped
1 cup pecans, chopped
16 ounces milk chocolate or
dark chocolate melting candy

Heat the butter and cream in a saucepan over low heat, stirring until the butter melts. Stir in the fondant powder. Knead to form a stiff dough. Mix in the cherries and pecans. Shape the mixture into 24 small balls.

Melt the chocolate in a double boiler over hot water. Drop each fondant ball into the chocolate using a teaspoon. Coat the ball, let excess chocolate drain and remove to waxed paper to harden. Let stand for several hours or freeze for 20 minutes. Wrap in candy paper or candy foils and store tightly covered. Makes 24 servings.

Toffee Crunch

$1/2$ cup (1 stick) butter or margarine
1 cup sugar
1 tablespoon water
1 tablespoon light corn syrup
$1/2$ cup toasted almonds, finely chopped
6 or 7 small Hershey's candy bars
$1/2$ cup whole toasted almonds

Combine the butter, sugar, water and corn syrup in a saucepan and mix well. Cook over medium heat to 295 degrees on a candy thermometer. Remove from the heat and stir in the chopped almonds. Spread quickly on a buttered baking sheet. Top with the candy bars and spread the chocolate as it melts. Sprinkle with the whole almonds. Chill until the candy is hard. Break into serving-size pieces. Makes 8 to 10 servings.

Chapter Recipes

Desserts & Sweets

Apple Pie Cake with Caramel Sauce

1/4 cup shortening
1 cup sugar
1 egg
2 tablespoons hot water
1 teaspoon vanilla extract
1 cup flour
1 teaspoon baking soda
1/2 teaspoon cinnamon
1/2 teaspoon nutmeg
1/4 teaspoon salt
1 1/2 cups chopped apples
1/2 cup chopped pecans
Caramel Sauce
Whipped cream

Beat the shortening and sugar in a mixing bowl until light and fluffy. Add the egg and mix well. Stir in the hot water and vanilla. Sift the flour, baking soda, cinnamon, nutmeg and salt together. Add to the creamed mixture and mix well. Stir in the apples and pecans. Pour into a greased 9-inch pie plate. Bake at 325 degrees for 45 minutes. Top each serving with Caramel Sauce and whipped cream. Makes 8 servings.

Caramel Sauce

1/2 cup (1 stick) butter
1 cup sugar
1/2 cup milk
1 teaspoon vanilla extract

Combine the butter, sugar, milk and vanilla in a saucepan. Bring to a boil. Reduce the heat and simmer for 10 minutes. Makes 1 cup.

Fresh Apple Cake with Toffee Cream

1/2 cup (1 stick) butter, softened
1 cup sugar
2 eggs, beaten
2 cups flour
2 teaspoons baking soda
1 teaspoon cinnamon
1/2 teaspoon nutmeg
6 Jonathan apples, peeled, chopped
1 cup chopped walnuts
Toffee Cream

Beat the butter and sugar in a mixing bowl until light and fluffy. Add the eggs and mix well. Sift the flour, baking soda, cinnamon and nutmeg together. Add to the creamed mixture and mix well. Stir in the apples and walnuts. Spoon the batter into a greased 8×12-inch glass baking dish. Bake at 325 degrees for 40 to 50 minutes or until the top springs back when touched. Serve the cake hot, topped with Toffee Cream. Makes 12 servings.

Toffee Cream

1 cup (2 sticks) butter
1 cup sugar
1 cup firmly packed brown sugar
1 cup sour cream
1 tablespoon vanilla extract

Combine the butter, sugar, brown sugar, sour cream and vanilla in a saucepan. Bring to a boil, stirring constantly. Serve warm. Makes 2 to 3 cups.

Note: *This rich sauce is delicious over ice cream and many other desserts. Store it in the refrigerator and warm in the microwave as needed.*

Irish Coffee Liqueur Chocolate Cake

3/4 cup (1 1/2 sticks) butter, softened
2 cups sugar
3/4 cup baking cocoa, sifted
4 eggs, separated
1 teaspoon baking soda
2 tablespoons cold water
1/2 cup cold coffee
1/2 cup Irish Coffee liqueur
1 3/4 cups sifted cake flour
2 teaspoons vanilla extract
1 cup confectioners' sugar
1 cup Irish Coffee liqueur
Grand Marnier Sauce
Apricot Sauce

Beat the butter and sugar in a mixing bowl until light and fluffy. Stir in the baking cocoa. Add the egg yolks 1 at a time, mixing well after each addition. Dissolve the baking soda in the water and combine with the coffee and 1/2 cup liqueur. Add to the creamed mixture alternately with the flour, beginning and ending with the flour. Stir in the vanilla. Fold in the stiffly beaten egg whites. Pour into a greased and floured bundt pan. Bake at 325 degrees for 45 minutes. Invert onto a serving plate. Combine the confectioners' sugar and 1 cup liqueur and spread over the warm cake. Let stand until cool. Store in the refrigerator. Top each serving with Grand Marnier Sauce and Apricot Sauce. Makes 12 to 16 servings.

Grand Marnier Sauce

1 cup whipping cream
1/2 cup sugar
3 teaspoons lemon juice
6 tablespoons Grand Marnier
1 teaspoon grated orange zest

Whip the cream in a bowl until stiff. Beat in the sugar, lemon juice, Grand Marnier and orange zest. Makes 2 cups.

Apricot Sauce

1 1/2 cups apricot jam
1/2 cup water
2 tablespoons sugar
1 to 2 tablespoons kirsch or brandy (optional)

Bring the apricot jam, water and sugar to a boil in a saucepan and reduce the heat. Simmer for 5 to 10 minutes, stirring constantly. Strain the sauce through a sieve and stir in the kirsch. Makes 2 cups.

Gingerbread with Brown Sugar Sauce

2 cups flour
1 cup sugar
4 teaspoons cinnamon
4 teaspoons ginger
1 teaspoon nutmeg
1 teaspoon baking soda
1/4 teaspoon salt
1 cup buttermilk
1 cup vegetable oil
1 cup dark molasses
2 eggs
Brown Sugar Sauce
Whipped cream

Combine the flour, sugar, cinnamon, ginger, nutmeg, baking soda and salt in a large mixing bowl. Add the buttermilk, oil, molasses and eggs. Beat at medium speed for 2 to 3 minutes or until smooth and creamy. Pour into a greased 9×13-inch baking pan. Bake at 325 degrees for 45 minutes. Top each serving with warm Brown Sugar Sauce and whipped cream. Makes 18 to 20 servings.

Brown Sugar Sauce

1/2 cup (1 stick) butter
1 cup firmly packed brown sugar
1 (12-ounce) can evaporated milk
2 teaspoons vanilla extract

Melt the butter in a saucepan over medium heat. Stir in the brown sugar. Cook until the sugar is dissolved, stirring constantly. Add the milk and vanilla slowly, stirring until well blended. Serve warm. Makes 2 cups.

Chocolate-Glazed Triple-Layer Cheesecake

The crumb crust

8 ounces chocolate wafer cookies, crushed

1/4 cup sugar

5 tablespoons butter, melted

For the crumb crust, combine the chocolate wafer crumbs, sugar and butter in a bowl and mix well. Press onto the bottom and 2 inches up the side of a 9-inch springform pan.

The chocolate layer

1 (8-ounce) package cream cheese, softened

1/4 cup sugar

1 egg

1/4 teaspoon vanilla extract

2 ounces semisweet chocolate, melted

1/3 cup sour cream

For the chocolate layer, combine the cream cheese and sugar in a mixing bowl. Beat at medium speed until fluffy. Beat in the egg and vanilla. Stir in the chocolate and sour cream. Spoon over the chocolate crust.

The pecan layer

1 (8-ounce) package cream cheese, softened

1/3 cup firmly packed dark brown sugar

1 tablespoon flour

1 egg

1/2 teaspoon vanilla extract

1/4 cup chopped pecans

For the pecan layer, combine the cream cheese, brown sugar and flour in a mixing bowl. Beat at medium speed until fluffy. Beat in the egg and vanilla. Stir in the pecans. Spoon over the chocolate layer.

The sour cream layer

5 ounces cream cheese, softened

1/4 cup sugar

1 egg

1 cup sour cream

1/4 teaspoon each vanilla and almond extract

Chocolate Glaze

Chocolate leaves (optional)

For the sour cream layer, beat the cream cheese and sugar at medium speed in a mixing bowl until fluffy. Beat in the egg. Add the sour cream and flavorings. Spoon over the pecan layer. Bake at 325 degrees for 1 hour. Turn off the oven and let stand for 30 minutes. Open the door and let stand for 30 minutes. Cool. Chill, covered, for 8 hours. Remove from the pan. Spread with Chocolate Glaze. Top with chocolate leaves. Makes 16 to 20 servings.

Chocolate Glaze

6 ounces semisweet chocolate
1/4 cup (1/2 stick) butter
3/4 cup sifted confectioners' sugar
2 tablespoons water
1 teaspoon vanilla extract

Combine the chocolate and butter in a double boiler over simmering water. Cook until the chocolate melts. Remove from the heat and add the confectioners' sugar, water and vanilla, stirring until smooth. Makes enough glaze for a 9-inch cake.

Black Russian Cake

1 package yellow cake mix
1 package chocolate instant pudding mix
1/4 cup vodka
1/4 cup Kahlúa
1 cup vegetable oil
1/2 cup sugar
3/4 cup water
4 eggs
1 cup confectioners' sugar
1/4 cup Kahlúa

Combine the cake mix, pudding mix, vodka, 1/4 cup Kahlúa, oil, sugar, water and eggs in a mixing bowl. Beat at high speed for 4 minutes or until smooth and creamy. Pour into a greased and floured bundt pan. Bake at 375 degrees for 45 to 50 minutes. Invert onto a serving plate and pierce holes into the top of the cake with a wooden pick. Combine the confectioners' sugar and 1/4 cup Kahlúa and pour over the warm cake. Makes 12 to 16 servings.

Note: *This cake tastes better the second day, which makes it a good make-ahead dessert.*

Three-Day Coconut Cake

1 (2-layer) package yellow butter cake mix
2 cups sugar
2 cups sour cream
1 (14-ounce) package shredded coconut
1 teaspoon vanilla extract
1 (12-ounce) container whipped topping

Prepare and bake the cake using the package directions for two 2-inch cake pans. Split the cooled layers horizontally. Combine the sugar, sour cream, coconut and vanilla in a bowl and mix well. Spread 1/2 of the filling between the layers. Add the whipped topping to the remaining filling and spread over the top and side of the cake. Chill for 3 days before serving. Makes 16 servings.

Angel Food Cake

12 egg whites, at room temperature
1 1/2 teaspoons cream of tartar
1/8 teaspoon salt
1 teaspoon vanilla extract
1/2 teaspoon almond extract
1 cup sugar
1 cup sifted cake flour
1/2 cup sugar

Beat the egg whites in a mixing bowl at low speed until foamy. Add the cream of tartar, salt, vanilla and almond extract. Beat at medium speed until soft peaks form. Add 1 cup sugar gradually, beating constantly at high speed until stiff peaks form. Combine the flour and 1/2 cup sugar and fold into the egg white mixture gently. Spoon into an ungreased tube pan. Place the cake in a cold oven and heat to 350 degrees. Bake for 1 hour or until the top is brown and dry. Invert on a funnel to cool completely. Loosen the cake from the side of the pan. Invert onto a cake plate. Remove the crust from the top and side before serving. Makes 12 servings.

Hot Milk Cake with Lemon Sauce

1/2 cup (1 stick) butter
1 cup milk
2 cups flour
2 tablespoons baking powder
Pinch of salt
4 eggs
2 cups sugar
1 teaspoon vanilla extract
1 teaspoon lemon juice
Lemon Sauce

Melt the butter with the milk in a saucepan. Bring to a boil and remove from the heat. Combine the flour, baking powder and salt in a bowl. Beat the eggs with the sugar in a large mixing bowl. Add the flour mixture and mix well. Beat in the butter mixture, vanilla and lemon juice. Pour into an ungreased tube pan. Bake at 300 degrees for 45 to 60 minutes. Cool in the pan for 15 to 20 minutes. Loosen the cake from the side of the pan. Cool completely and invert onto a serving plate. Top each serving with warm Lemon Sauce.
Makes 18 to 24 servings.

Lemon Sauce

1/2 cup sugar
1 tablespoon cornstarch
Dash of salt
Dash of nutmeg
1 cup water
2 tablespoons butter
1 1/2 tablespoons lemon juice

Combine the sugar, cornstarch, salt and nutmeg in a saucepan and stir in the water. Cook over medium heat until thick and clear, stirring constantly. Stir in the butter and lemon juice and blend well. Serve warm. Makes 1 cup.

Hibiscus Nectar Cake

1/2 cup (1 stick) butter, softened
1/2 cup shortening
2 cups sugar
5 eggs, separated
1 1/4 teaspoons vanilla extract
1 teaspoon coconut extract
1 cup buttermilk
1/4 cup sour cream
2 cups flour
1 teaspoon baking soda
1/2 teaspoon salt
2 cups shredded coconut
1 cup pecans, chopped
1/2 cup maraschino cherries, drained, chopped
Cherry Nut Frosting

Cream the butter and shortening in a mixing bowl until fluffy. Beat in the sugar gradually. Add the egg yolks 1 at a time, mixing well after each addition. Stir in the vanilla and coconut extract. Combine the buttermilk and sour cream in a small bowl and mix well. Combine the flour, baking soda and salt in a bowl and mix well. Add to the creamed mixture alternately with the buttermilk mixture, beginning and ending with the flour mixture. Fold in the stiffly beaten egg whites. Fold in the coconut, pecans and cherries. Pour into 3 greased and floured 9-inch cake pans. Bake at 350 degrees for 20 minutes. Cool in the pans for 10 minutes. Remove to a wire rack to cool completely. Spread the Cherry Nut Frosting between the layers and over the top and side of the cooled cake. Makes 16 servings.

Cherry Nut Frosting

1/2 cup (1 stick) butter, softened
1 (8-ounce) package cream cheese, softened
1 teaspoon vanilla extract
1/2 teaspoon coconut extract
1 (1-pound) package confectioners' sugar
1 cup chopped pecans
1/2 cup maraschino cherries, drained, chopped

Cream the butter and cream cheese at medium speed in a mixing bowl. Mix in the vanilla and coconut extract. Beat in the confectioners' sugar gradually. Fold in the pecans and cherries. Makes enough frosting for a 3-layer cake.

Sticky Toffee Pudding Cake

2 1/4 cups pitted dates
2 cups water
2 teaspoons baking soda
2 teaspoons vanilla extract
1/2 cup (1 stick) butter, softened
1 1/2 cups sugar
2 eggs
4 cups flour
1 teaspoon baking powder
Pinch of salt
Toffee Sauce
Whipped cream

Combine the dates and water in a saucepan and bring to a boil. Reduce the heat and simmer for 2 to 3 minutes. Strain the dates, reserving the liquid. Peel and chop the dates. Combine the dates and reserved liquid in the saucepan and bring to a boil. Cool slightly. Stir in the baking soda and vanilla.

Cream the butter and sugar in a bowl until light and fluffy. Beat in the eggs 1 at a time. Sift the flour, baking powder and salt together. Add to the creamed mixture alternately with the undrained dates, beating well after each addition. Spoon into ten 4-ounce muffin cups coated with nonstick cooking spray. Cover with waxed paper and a baking sheet. Bake at 325 degrees for 15 minutes or until brown and firm. Cool in the pan and remove to a wire rack.

Fill each muffin cup 1/4 full with Toffee Sauce and top with a cake. Chill or freeze until serving time. Remove from the cups and warm in the microwave, adding more Toffee Sauce if desired. Top with whipped cream. Makes 10 servings.

Toffee Sauce

1/2 cup (1 stick) butter
1 (1-pound) box brown sugar
2 cups heavy cream
2 tablespoons rum or brandy

Melt the butter with the brown sugar in a saucepan. Stir in the cream and bring to a full boil. Remove from the heat and let cool for a few minutes. Stir in the rum. Serve warm. Makes 3 cups.

Almond Cake with Raspberry Sauce

1 (8-ounce) can almond paste
1/2 cup (1 stick) butter, softened
3/4 cup sugar
3 eggs
1 tablespoon kirsch
1/3 teaspoon baking powder
1/4 cup flour
Confectioners' sugar to taste
1 pint fresh raspberries, or 12 ounces
unsweetened frozen raspberries, thawed
2 tablespoons sugar

Cream the almond paste, butter and 3/4 cup sugar in a mixing bowl until light and fluffy. Add the eggs, kirsch, baking powder and flour and beat just until smooth. Pour into a buttered and floured 8-inch cake pan. Bake at 350 degrees for 40 to 50 minutes. Cool in the pan for 10 minutes. Remove to a wire rack to cool completely. Dust with confectioners' sugar. Combine the raspberries and 2 tablespoons sugar in a blender and process until smooth. Strain the purée through a sieve and discard the seeds. Spoon purée on each dessert plate and top with a slice of the almond cake. Makes 10 servings.

Fresh Berry Gratin

3 cups fresh berries (raspberries, blueberries
and/or blackberries)
4 ounces reduced-fat cream cheese, softened
3 tablespoons skim milk
1 tablespoon lemon juice
1/3 cup firmly packed light brown sugar

Spread the berries in an even layer in a buttered 9-inch pie plate or 4 individual gratin dishes. Whisk the cream cheese, milk and lemon juice together in a small bowl. Spread over the berries, leaving the outer edge uncovered. Chill, covered, for up to 1 hour. Press the brown sugar through a coarse sieve over the berries, covering them evenly. Broil for 4 minutes or until the sugar is melted. Makes 4 servings.

Apple Crisp

6 or 7 large green apples, peeled,
cut into 1-inch cubes
1/4 cup water
1 tablespoon lemon juice
1 1/2 cups firmly packed brown sugar
1 1/2 cups flour
1 cup rolled oats
1 1/2 teaspoons ginger
2 tablespoons cinnamon
1/2 teaspoon nutmeg
1 cup (2 sticks) butter, cut into 1/2-inch cubes
1/2 cup chopped pecans

Combine the apples, water and lemon juice in a large bowl and mix well. Spread in a buttered 9×13-inch baking dish. Mix the brown sugar, flour, oats, ginger, cinnamon and nutmeg in a bowl. Cut in the butter until crumbly. Stir in the pecans. Spoon over the apples and pat the topping down lightly. Bake at 375 degrees for 45 minutes or until the topping is golden brown and the apples are bubbly. Serve warm with ice cream. Makes 6 to 8 servings.

Peanut Butter Pie

1 (8-ounce) package cream cheese, softened
1 cup confectioners' sugar
3/4 cup peanut butter
2 to 3 tablespoons milk
1 (9-ounce) carton whipped topping
1 (9-inch) graham cracker crust
1/4 cup chopped peanuts (optional)

Cream the cream cheese and sugar in a large bowl until light and fluffy. Add the peanut butter and blend well. Beat in the milk a little at a time. Fold in the whipped topping. Spoon into the pie shell and sprinkle with the chopped peanuts. Chill for several hours or freeze. Makes 6 to 8 servings.

Cranberry Pear Crisp

2 cups cranberries
2 large pears, peeled, cored, sliced
1/4 cup sugar
3/4 teaspoon cinnamon
1/4 teaspoon nutmeg
3/4 cup sifted flour
3/4 cup rolled oats
3/4 cup firmly packed dark brown sugar
3/4 cup (1 1/2 sticks) unsalted butter,
cut into pieces
3/4 cup chopped pecans

Combine the cranberries and pears in a large bowl. Add the sugar, cinnamon and nutmeg and mix well. Pour into a buttered 9×11-inch baking dish. Combine the flour, oats and brown sugar in a bowl. Cut in the butter until crumbly. Stir in the pecans. Spread the topping evenly over the fruit. Bake at 350 degrees for 35 to 40 minutes or until the juices are bubbly and the topping is golden brown. Makes 8 to 10 servings.

Harvest Fruit and Nut Pie

1 (2-crust) pie pastry
4 medium Granny Smith apples, peeled, sliced
1 cup cranberries
1/2 cup golden raisins
1/2 cup chopped walnuts or pecans
1 cup sugar
2/3 cup firmly packed brown sugar
1/4 cup flour
1 teaspoon cinnamon
1/4 teaspoon nutmeg
3 tablespoons butter
1 tablespoon sugar
1/2 teaspoon cinnamon

Fit the bottom pastry into a pie plate and trim the edge. Combine the apples, cranberries, raisins, walnuts, 1 cup sugar, brown sugar, flour, 1 teaspoon cinnamon and nutmeg in a large bowl and mix well. Pour into the pie shell. Dot with the butter. Fit the top pastry over the pie and seal. Prick with a fork. Combine 1 tablespoon sugar and 1/2 teaspoon cinnamon and sprinkle over the pie. Bake at 400 degrees for 45 minutes or until the pie tests done. Serve with vanilla ice cream. Makes 8 servings.

Sour Cream Pumpkin Pie

The crust

1 1/2 cups graham cracker crumbs
1/2 cup confectioners' sugar
1/2 cup (1 stick) butter, melted

The filling

12 ounces cream cheese, softened
3/4 cup sugar
1 1/2 tablespoons flour
1 teaspoon grated orange zest
1 teaspoon grated lemon zest
2 eggs plus 2 egg yolks
1 cup fresh cooked or canned pumpkin
1/8 teaspoon cinnamon

The topping

2 cups sour cream
3 tablespoons sugar
1 teaspoon vanilla extract
Sour cream

For the crust, mix the graham cracker crumbs, confectioners' sugar and butter in a bowl. Press into a 9-inch pie plate and sprinkle lightly with water. Bake at 300 degrees for 8 minutes.

For the filling, combine the cream cheese, sugar, flour, orange zest and lemon zest in a mixing bowl and mix well. Add the eggs and egg yolks and beat at medium speed until smooth. Stir in the pumpkin and cinnamon. Pour into the crumb crust. Bake at 350 degrees for 40 minutes or until set.

For the topping, combine 2 cups sour cream, the sugar and vanilla and spread over the pie. Bake for 10 minutes longer. Cool completely. Spread with a thin layer of cold sour cream.
Makes 8 to 10 servings.

Coconut Cream Tarts with Macadamia Nut Crust

The coconut cream
1/3 cup flour
3/4 cup sugar
4 eggs
2 cups milk
1 tablespoon vanilla extract
1 1/2 cups shredded coconut

For the coconut cream, combine the flour and sugar in a bowl. Stir in the eggs. Heat the milk in a heavy saucepan over medium heat just until hot. Stir a small amount of the hot milk into the egg mixture; stir the egg mixture into the remaining hot milk in the saucepan. Cook over medium heat for 5 to 6 minutes or until the mixture thickens, stirring constantly. Remove from the heat. Stir in the vanilla and 1 cup of the coconut. Chill, covered, for 3 hours. Bake the remaining 1/2 cup coconut on a baking sheet at 350 degrees for 5 minutes or until toasted.

The macadamia nut crust
2 1/2 cups flour
3/4 cup (1 1/2 sticks) cold butter, cut into pieces
2 tablespoons water
1 1/2 cups macadamia nuts, chopped
Whipped cream

For the macadamia nut crust, combine the flour and butter in a mixer fitted with a dough hook and mix until crumbly. Add the water and process until the mixture forms a ball. Knead the macadamia nuts into the dough on a lightly floured surface. Divide the dough into 12 equal portions. Press each portion into a 3- or 4-inch tart pan and prick the bottom with a fork. Place the tarts on a jelly roll pan and freeze, covered, for 30 minutes or more. Bake at 375 degrees for 15 to 20 minutes. Cool in the pans for 5 minutes. Remove the tarts from the pans to a wire rack to cool completely. Spoon the coconut cream into the shells. Top with whipped cream and the toasted coconut. Makes 12 servings.

Chocolate Tartlets

1/2 cup (1 stick) butter, softened
1 (3-ounce) package cream cheese, softened
1 cup flour
1 (4-ounce) bar sweet cooking chocolate, broken into pieces
3 tablespoons hot water
1 teaspoon vanilla extract
1 cup whipping cream
1/4 cup sugar
1/2 teaspoon vanilla extract

Cream the butter and cream cheese in a mixing bowl until fluffy. Stir in the flour. Chill, covered, for 1 hour or until the dough is easy to handle. Shape into 1-inch balls. Press on the bottom and up the side of 24 ungreased 1 3/4-inch muffin cups. Bake at 325 degrees for 25 minutes or until done. Cool slightly in the pan. Remove to a wire rack to cool completely. Combine the chocolate and hot water in a saucepan over low heat. Cook until the chocolate is melted, stirring constantly. Cool to room temperature. Stir in 1 teaspoon vanilla. Whip the cream with the sugar and 1/2 teaspoon vanilla in a bowl until stiff peaks form. Fold into the chocolate mixture. Spoon into the tart shells.
Makes 24 servings.

Chocolate-Kissed Heavenly Fruit

4 medium navel oranges, peeled, sliced, drained
1 cup sliced strawberries
3 bananas, sliced
1 cup whipping cream, chilled
2 tablespoons sugar
1 tablespoon orange liqueur
1 cup grated semisweet chocolate
Strawberries

Layer the fruits in a 9×13-inch glass baking dish or in individual soufflé dishes. Whip the cream with the sugar in a mixing bowl until well combined. Add the liqueur and beat until stiff peaks form. Spread over the fruit. Sprinkle with the grated chocolate, covering the cream completely. Broil 5 inches from the heat source for 2 to 3 minutes or until the chocolate melts, being careful that the chocolate does not burn. Top each serving with a strawberry.
Makes 6 to 8 servings.

Frozen Chocolate Sundae

24 chocolate sandwich cookies, crushed
1/4 cup (1/2 stick) margarine, melted
1/2 gallon vanilla ice cream, softened
12 ounces semisweet chocolate chips
1/2 cup (1 stick) margarine, melted
2 cups confectioners' sugar
1 (12-ounce) can evaporated milk
1 teaspoon vanilla extract
1 small container whipped topping
Maraschino cherries
1/2 cup chopped nuts

Combine the cookie crumbs and 1/4 cup margarine in a small bowl and mix well. Press in a 9×13-inch baking dish. Freeze until firm. Spread the ice cream over the crumb crust and freeze until firm. Combine the chocolate chips, 1/2 cup margarine, confectioners' sugar and evaporated milk in a saucepan. Bring to a boil. Boil for 8 minutes, stirring constantly. Remove from the heat and stir in the vanilla. Cool to room temperature. Spread over the ice cream and freeze until firm. Top each serving with whipped topping, a cherry and nuts. Makes 12 servings.

Brownie Trifle

1 package fudge brownie mix
1/4 cup praline- or coffee-flavor
liqueur (optional)
1 large package chocolate instant pudding mix,
or 2 packages chocolate instant
mousse mix
8 (1-ounce) Heath bars or Skor bars, crushed
1 (12-ounce) container whipped
topping, thawed
Chocolate curls or crushed Heath bars

Prepare and bake the brownie mix using the package directions. Prick the warm brownie at 1-inch intervals with a meat fork and brush with the liqueur. Let cool completely; crumble. Prepare the pudding mix using the package directions, omitting the chilling. Sprinkle 1/2 of the brownie crumbs in the bottom of a 3-quart trifle dish. Top with 1/2 of the pudding, 1/2 of the crushed candy bars and 1/2 of the whipped topping. Repeat the layers with the remaining ingredients. Garnish with chocolate curls or crushed Heath bars. Chill for 8 hours. Makes 16 to 18 servings.

Coffee Ice Cream Dessert

2 packages ladyfingers
3 tablespoons instant coffee granules
3 tablespoons boiling water
1/2 gallon vanilla ice cream, softened
2 1/2 boxes small Heath Bar Crunch candy bars, crushed
1 to 2 cups whipping cream
2 1/2 jiggers clear crème de cacao

Line the bottom and side of a springform pan with the ladyfingers. Dissolve the instant coffee granules in the water. Add to the ice cream and mix well. Stir in 3/4 of the crushed candy bars. Pour into the lined pan. Freeze until firm. Whip the cream in a mixing bowl until soft peaks form. Beat in the crème de cacao. Spread over the ice cream and sprinkle with the remaining crushed candy bars.
Makes 8 to 10 servings.

Three Sisters Ice Cream

1 1/2 cups fresh orange juice (about 3 oranges)
3/4 cup fresh lemon juice (about 3 lemons)
1 1/2 cups mashed bananas (3 to 4 bananas)
3 cups half-and-half
2 cups sugar

Combine the orange juice, lemon juice, bananas, half-and-half and sugar in an ice cream freezer container. Freeze using the manufacturer's directions. Makes 4 quarts, or 25 to 30 servings.

Crème Brûlée

8 egg yolks
3/4 cup sugar
2 cups heavy cream
2 cups milk
1 vanilla bean, cut in half
6 to 7 teaspoons raw sugar

Beat the egg yolks and 1/2 of the sugar in a mixing bowl until pale yellow. Combine the cream, milk, vanilla bean and remaining sugar in a saucepan. Bring to a boil and remove from the heat. Add 1/2 of the cream mixture slowly to the egg mixture, whisking constantly. Stir in the remaining cream mixture. Ladle into ten 4-ounce ramekins. Place the ramekins in a 10×15-inch baking pan and cover with a sheet of waxed paper. Place in a 300-degree oven. Pour 1 to 1 1/2 quarts hot water into the pan to a depth of 1/4 inch. Place another baking pan over the waxed paper. Bake for 45 minutes. Cool completely. Chill until serving time.

Sprinkle with the raw sugar. Broil until the sugar melts and caramelizes or caramelize the sugar with a kitchen propane torch. Chill until serving time. Makes 10 servings.

Presentation can always enhance the appeal of a dessert. Garnishes made with chocolate are some of the easiest to master. For a quick chocolate drizzle, melt chocolate in a microwave and then pour into a plastic bag and seal. Snip a small corner of the bag to allow a small drizzle to escape. You can drizzle chocolate over an entire dessert, individual servings, or individual serving plates. You can also drizzle chocolate onto waxed paper into desired shapes. When cooled and hardened, remove from the waxed paper and place on the dessert. To make chocolate leaves, brush melted chocolate onto the backs of clean, nonpoisonous leaves. When hardened, carefully peel away the leaves.

No-Bake Crème Brûlée with Raspberry Sauce

6 egg yolks
1/2 cup sugar
1 1/2 cups heavy cream
1 vanilla bean, split lengthwise
1 cup raspberries
2 (10-ounce) packages frozen puff pastry shells, thawed, baked
1/3 cup firmly packed brown sugar
Raspberry Sauce

Beat the egg yolks in a mixing bowl at high speed for 3 minutes or until thick and pale yellow. Beat in the sugar gradually. Heat the cream and vanilla bean in a saucepan over medium heat just until hot. Strain through a fine sieve; discard the vanilla bean. Stir 1/2 of the hot cream gradually into the egg yolk mixture; stir the egg yolk mixture into the remaining hot cream in the saucepan. Cook over low heat for 5 to 8 minutes or until the mixture thickens, stirring constantly and not allowing the custard to boil. Chill, covered, for 3 or more hours.

Place 2 raspberries in each pastry shell and fill with the custard. Chill until serving time. Sprinkle a heaping teaspoon of the brown sugar over each shell. Broil 5 inches from the heat source for 2 to 4 minutes or just until the sugar begins to melt. Pour Raspberry Sauce onto 12 dessert plates. Top with a filled pastry shell and serve immediately. Makes 12 servings.

Raspberry Sauce

1/2 cup sugar
1/2 cup water
2 cups raspberries

Bring the sugar and water to a boil in a heavy 1-quart saucepan. Boil for 2 minutes or until the sugar is dissolved, stirring frequently. Cool. Purée the raspberries in a blender. Strain through a fine sieve and discard the seeds. Add the raspberry purée to the sugar syrup and stir well. Makes 1 1/2 cups.

Chocolate-Dipped Cherry Cordials

1 cup maraschino cherries with stems, drained
1 cup brandy
10 ounces semisweet chocolate

Combine the cherries and brandy in a bowl. Let stand for 8 to 10 hours. Drain the cherries and freeze. Melt the chocolate in a double boiler over simmering water. Wipe each frozen cherry to remove excess moisture. Dip in the melted chocolate and let stand on waxed paper until firm. Store in the refrigerator. Makes about 18 servings, or 36 cherries.

Millionaire Fudge

$4^1/2$ cups sugar
1 (12-ounce) can evaporated milk
$^1/2$ cup (1 stick) butter
$^1/2$ teaspoon salt
2 large (1-pound) Hershey bars, broken into pieces
12 ounces semisweet chocolate chips
1 jar marshmallow cream
2 to 4 cups pecans, broken
2 teaspoons vanilla extract

Combine the sugar, evaporated milk, butter and salt in a saucepan. Bring to a boil, stirring constantly. Boil gently for 10 minutes, stirring constantly. Remove from the heat. Add the chocolate bars, chocolate chips and marshmallow cream and stir until smooth. Add the pecans and vanilla. Pour into a buttered baking pan. Let stand, covered, at room temperature for 8 to 10 hours. Cut into squares and wrap in foil. Makes 25 servings.

Note: *This smooth and creamy fudge is pretty at Christmastime wrapped in different colors of foil. You will find the foil in craft stores.*

Brown Sugar Cookies

1 cup shortening or 1 cup (2 sticks) margarine
1^1/$_2$ cups firmly packed brown sugar
^{3}/$_4$ cup sugar
2 eggs
3^1/$_2$ cups flour
^{1}/$_4$ teaspoon salt
1 teaspoon baking soda
1 teaspoon cream of tartar
2 tablespoons cream
1 tablespoon vanilla extract
1^1/$_2$ cups nuts

Cream the shortening, brown sugar and sugar in a bowl until light and fluffy. Add the eggs and mix well. Add a mixture of the flour, salt, baking soda and cream of tartar and mix well. Stir in the cream and vanilla. Add the nuts. Drop by teaspoonfuls onto a nonstick cookie sheet. Bake at 350 degrees until brown. Cool on a wire rack. Makes 5 to 7 dozen.

Chocolate Chunk Walnut Cookies

1 cup (2 sticks) unsalted butter, softened
1 cup sugar
1^1/$_2$ teaspoons vanilla extract
1 teaspoon salt
2 cups flour
1 pound semisweet chocolate, cut into
^{1}/$_2$-inch pieces
1 cup coarsely chopped walnuts

Cream the butter and sugar in a mixing bowl until light and fluffy. Stir in the vanilla and salt. Add the flour, chocolate pieces and walnuts and mix well. Shape into golf ball-size balls and place 2 inches apart on a cookie sheet. Bake at 350 degrees for 10 to 15 minutes or until the edges are light brown. Cool on a wire rack. Makes about 2 dozen.

Note: *Try using white chocolate and dried cranberries in this recipe.*

To-Die-For Chocolate Chip Cookies

1 cup (2 sticks) unsalted butter, softened
3/4 cup each sugar and packed brown sugar
1 tablespoon vanilla extract
1 tablespoon Frangelico (hazelnut liqueur)
1 tablespoon coffee liqueur
2 eggs
2 1/2 cups flour
1 teaspoon baking soda
1/2 teaspoon salt
12 ounces milk chocolate chips
1 cup chopped walnuts
1/2 cup chopped pecans
1/2 cup chopped macadamia nuts

Combine the butter, sugar, brown sugar, vanilla, Frangelico and coffee liqueur in a mixing bowl and beat until light and fluffy. Add the eggs and mix well. Add a mixture of the flour, baking soda and salt and mix well. Stir in the chocolate chips, walnuts, pecans and macadamia nuts. Drop by 1/4 cupfuls onto an ungreased cookie sheet, spacing the cookies well apart. Bake at 325 degrees for 16 minutes or until golden brown. Remove to a wire rack to cool. Makes 3 dozen.

Chocolate Fudge Cookies

9 ounces (1 1/2 cups) semisweet chocolate chips
2 tablespoons butter
1 cup flour
1 cup chopped walnuts
1 (14-ounce) can sweetened condensed milk

Melt the chocolate chips and butter in a double boiler over simmering water. Reduce the heat to low and stir in the flour, walnuts and condensed milk. Drop by rounded tablespoonfuls onto a greased cookie sheet. Bake at 325 degrees for 8 to 10 minutes. Cool on a wire rack. Makes 3 dozen.

Peanut Butter Cookies

1/2 cup shortening
1/2 cup peanut butter
1/2 cup sugar
1/2 cup firmly packed brown sugar
1 egg
1 1/4 cups sifted flour
3/4 teaspoon baking soda
1/2 teaspoon baking powder
1/4 teaspoon salt
Sugar to taste

Cream the shortening and peanut butter in a mixing bowl until smooth. Add the sugar and brown sugar and cream until light and fluffy. Add the egg and mix well. Sift the flour, baking soda, baking powder and salt together and add to the creamed mixture. Chill the dough until firm. Shape into balls and place on an ungreased cookie sheet. Flatten the balls with the bottom of a glass spread with shortening and dipped in additional sugar. Bake at 375 degrees for 8 to 10 minutes. Cool on a wire rack. Makes 4 to 5 dozen.

Crispy Pecan Cookies

1 cup shortening
1/2 cup (1 stick) margarine
1 cup sugar
1 cup firmly packed brown sugar
2 eggs
2 teaspoons vanilla extract
2 cups flour
1 teaspoon baking powder
1 teaspoon baking soda
1 teaspoon salt
2 1/2 cups rolled oats
1 cup chopped pecans
3 cups crisp rice cereal
1 1/2 cups shredded coconut

Cream the shortening, margarine, sugar and brown sugar in a mixing bowl until light and fluffy. Add the eggs and vanilla and mix well. Sift the flour, baking powder, baking soda and salt and add to the creamed mixture. Stir in the oats, pecans, rice cereal and coconut. Shape into balls and place on an ungreased cookie sheet. Bake at 350 degrees for 10 to 15 minutes. Cool on a wire rack. Makes 5 to 6 dozen.

Note: *These cookies are delicious with raisins added, and for a spicier version, add some cinnamon and nutmeg.*

Peanut Butter Brownies

1/3 cup butter or margarine
1/2 cup peanut butter
1 cup sugar
1/4 cup firmly packed brown sugar
2 eggs
1 cup flour
1 teaspoon baking powder
1/4 teaspoon salt
1/2 teaspoon vanilla extract
1 can of milk chocolate frosting or
other favorite chocolate frosting

Cream the butter, peanut butter, sugar and brown sugar in a mixing bowl until light and fluffy. Add the egg and mix well. Combine the flour, baking powder and salt and stir into the creamed mixture. Stir in the vanilla. Spread in a greased 9×9-inch baking pan. Bake at 350 degrees for 25 to 30 minutes. Cool in the pan. Spread the frosting on the cooled cake. Cut into bars. Makes 9 to 12 servings.

Lemon Bars

1/2 cup (1 stick) butter
2 cups sifted flour
1/2 cup confectioners' sugar
4 eggs, beaten
2 cups sugar
1/4 cup flour
6 tablespoons lemon juice
1/2 cup flaked coconut
Grated zest of 2 lemons
1 teaspoon baking powder
1/2 teaspoon salt
Confectioners' sugar to taste

Combine the butter, 2 cups flour and 1/2 cup confectioners' sugar in a mixing bowl and mix well. Press into a 9×13-inch baking pan. Bake at 350 degrees for 20 minutes. Combine the eggs, sugar, 1/4 cup flour, lemon juice, coconut, lemon zest, baking powder and salt in a mixing bowl and mix well. Spread over the hot crust. Bake for 30 minutes longer or until the center is barely set. Loosen the cake from the sides of the pan. Sprinkle with additional confectioners' sugar. Cool in the pan. Cut into bars. Makes 20 to 24 servings.

Pecan Toffee Squares

1 package Pillsbury moist supreme
yellow cake mix
1/2 cup (1 stick) butter or margarine, softened
1 egg
1 (14-ounce) can sweetened condensed milk
1 teaspoon vanilla extract
1 egg
1 (6-ounce) package chocolate-coated
toffee bits (Heath)
1 cup chopped pecans

Combine the cake mix, butter and 1 egg in a mixing bowl and mix well. Press into the bottom of a greased 9×13-inch baking pan. Bake at 350 degrees for 7 minutes.

Combine the condensed milk, vanilla and 1 egg and mix well. Stir in the toffee bits and pecans. Pour over the warm baked layer. Bake for 22 to 30 minutes longer or until the filling is set. Let stand for 1 hour or until completely cool. Cut into bars. Store in the refrigerator. Makes 24 to 36 servings.

Raspberry Dream Bars

1 1/2 cups flour
1 cup firmly packed brown sugar
1 teaspoon salt
2 cups quick-cooking oats
1 cup (2 sticks) unsalted butter
1 1/2 cups seedless raspberry jam
1/2 cup chopped pecans
1/2 cup or more semisweet chocolate chips,
melted (optional)

Combine the flour, brown sugar, salt and oats in a mixing bowl and mix well. Cut in the butter, reserving 2 tablespoons for the topping. Press 1/2 of the crumb mixture into the bottom of a greased 9×13-inch baking pan. Spread the raspberry jam over the crumb layer. Spread the remaining crumb mixture over the jam. Dot with the reserved butter and sprinkle with the pecans. Bake at 375 degrees for 20 to 25 minutes. Cool completely. Cut into bars. Drizzle with the melted chocolate before serving. Makes 24 servings.

Grandmother's Icebox Cookies

2 cups (4 sticks) unsalted butter
2$^{1}/_{2}$ cups sugar
3 eggs, lightly beaten
1 tablespoon light corn syrup
1 teaspoon vanilla extract
1 teaspoon baking soda
$^{1}/_{2}$ teaspoon salt
5$^{1}/_{2}$ cups flour
1 cup chopped pecans

Cream the butter and sugar in a large mixing bowl until light and fluffy. Add the eggs, corn syrup and vanilla and mix well. Combine the baking soda, salt and 1 cup of the flour and add to the creamed mixture. Add the remaining flour gradually, mixing well after each addition. Stir in the pecans. Shape the dough into 4 logs. Chill, tightly wrapped, in the refrigerator for at least 3 hours or freeze for up to 2 months. Cut into $^{1}/_{4}$-inch slices. Place on a greased cookie sheet. Bake at 350 degrees for 8 to 12 minutes or until the edges are brown. Cool on a wire rack. Makes 7 dozen.

Chewy Brownies

1$^{1}/_{2}$ cups flour
2 cups sugar
8 tablespoons baking cocoa
1 teaspoon salt
1 cup vegetable oil
4 eggs
2 tablespoons corn syrup
2 teaspoons vanilla extract
1 cup chopped pecans or walnuts

Combine the flour, sugar, baking cocoa, salt, oil, eggs, corn syrup, vanilla and pecans in a large mixing bowl. Beat by hand until smooth and creamy. Pour into a buttered 7×11-inch glass baking dish. Bake at 350 degrees for 30 minutes. Makes 16 servings.

Pumpkin Harvest Cookies

1 cup (2 sticks) butter, softened
1 1/2 cups firmly packed brown sugar
2 eggs
1 cup pumpkin
1 teaspoon vanilla extract
2 1/4 cups flour
1/2 teaspoon pumpkin pie spice
1/4 teaspoon baking soda
10 ounces white chocolate chips
1 cup chopped toasted pecans

Cream the butter and brown sugar in a large mixing bowl until light and fluffy. Add the eggs and mix well. Stir in the pumpkin and vanilla. Combine the flour, pumpkin pie spice and baking soda and add to the creamed mixture. Stir in the white chocolate chips and pecans. Drop by tablespoonfuls onto a greased cookie sheet. Bake at 300 degrees for 20 to 22 minutes. Cool on a wire rack. Makes 2 dozen.

Pumpkins Are Not Just for Carving

Too many people miss the delicious flavor of pumpkins by using them only for decoration. Ninety-nine percent of all pumpkins sold in America are used for decoration. The next time you plan to make a batch of pumpkin muffins or cookies, try using some freshly cooked pumpkin. To cook your own, choose small pumpkins and bake the cleaned halves, cut side down, in a baking pan at 325 degrees for 45 minutes or until tender. Peel and purée the pulp in a food processor.

Jan Hagels

1 cup (2 sticks) butter, softened
1 cup sugar
1 egg, separated
2 cups flour
1 teaspoon cinnamon
1 teaspoon vanilla extract
1 tablespoon water
1/2 cup finely chopped pecans

Cream the butter, sugar and egg yolk in a mixing bowl until light and fluffy. Add the flour, cinnamon and vanilla and mix well. Spread the dough evenly in a 10×15-inch baking pan coated with nonstick cooking spray. Beat the egg white with the water in a mixing bowl until frothy. Pour over the dough and spread evenly over the entire surface using the fingertips. Sprinkle with the pecans. Bake at 350 degrees for 25 to 30 minutes or until light brown. Cut into strips immediately using a pizza cutter. Cool on a wire rack. Makes about 40 servings.

Note: *These Dutch cookies, pronounced "yahn haggles," are often flavored with almond extract.*

Soccer Brownies

2 eggs, lightly beaten
1 cup sugar
1/2 cup (1 stick) butter, melted
2 squares unsweetened chocolate, melted
3/4 cup sifted flour
1/2 teaspoon salt
1 cup chopped pecans or walnuts
1 teaspoon vanilla extract
Confectioners' sugar (optional)

Combine the eggs and sugar in a mixing bowl and mix well. Stir in the butter and chocolate. Combine the flour, salt and pecans and add to the chocolate mixture. Stir in the vanilla. Pour into a buttered 9×9-inch baking pan. Bake at 325 degrees for 40 minutes. Cool in the pan and cut into squares. Sprinkle with confectioners' sugar. Makes 16 to 20 servings.

Chocolate Sherry Bars

The chocolate layer

4 ounces unsweetened chocolate
1 cup (2 sticks) butter or margarine
4 eggs
2 cups sugar
1 cup flour
1/4 teaspoon salt
1 teaspoon vanilla extract

The sherry filling

2 to 3 cups confectioners' sugar
1/4 cup (1/2 stick) butter or margarine, softened
1/4 cup sherry
1 tablespoon milk
1 cup chopped pecans

The topping

3 ounces semisweet chocolate chips
2 tablespoons butter or margarine
1 1/2 tablespoons water

For the chocolate layer, melt the chocolate and butter in a heavy saucepan over very low heat, stirring constantly. Cool slightly. Beat the eggs and sugar together in a mixing bowl. Stir in the chocolate mixture. Add the flour, salt and vanilla. Beat for 1 minute or until smooth and creamy. Pour into a greased 10×14-inch baking pan. Bake at 325 degrees for 45 minutes. Cool in the pan.

For the filling, combine the confectioners' sugar, butter, sherry and milk in a mixing bowl and mix until a spreading consistency. Stir in the pecans. Spread over the baked cake.

For the topping, combine the chocolate chips, butter and water in a saucepan. Heat over low heat until melted, stirring constantly. Drizzle over the cake filling. Chill thoroughly. Cut into bars. Makes 18 to 24 servings.

Recipe Contributors

We express our heartfelt appreciation to the members and friends who shared their delicious recipes for *Tailgates to Tea Parties*. Each recipe has been tested for accuracy and excellence. We regret that space limitations and duplications prevented us from including all the recipes that were submitted. Please accept our apologies if we have inadvertently excluded any recipe contributor.

Dot Adkins	Carolyn Glad	Kirsten Plusquellec
Lisa Allen	Karen Goins	Susan Potts
Jerrie Anderson	Nancy Gray	Janet Preble
Sandra Ayres	Kathe Green	Chris Purcell
Dolores Baer	Julie Baer Hall	Carole Pyle
Mignon Merchant Ball	Marilyn Hammond	Jane Remy
Kathy Barrett	Jill Hazeldine	Jaclynn Reynolds
Mona Barringer	Sandra Hook	Natalie Rice
Judy Barry	Susan Hosler	Pat Richardson
Dianne Bauman	L. Sue Hoy	Beth Ridgway
Leslie Baumert	Jamie Hubbard	Dana Rieger
Anita Bednar	Donna Hughes	Frances Ritchey
Jack Beller	Dot Hunt	Carolyn Rodgers
Ruth Beller	Simon Hurst	Brenda Runkle
Jane Benedum	Cindy Johnson	Jeri Saliba
Susan Bergen	Dorothea Johnson	Karen Sampson
Debby Bowman	Dorothy Johnson	Frances Sanger
Joyce Brandes	Lori Kennedy	Janice Scaramucci
Cindy Bryant	Paula Kopecky	Jill Schaefer
Nancy Burton	Kay Laffoon	Carolyn Schmidt
Donna Buwick	Juli Lane	Judy Scott
Jennifer Bynum	Sherry Latham	Jackie Shrode
Karla Campbell	Dorothy Lilly	Lee Smith
Sue Carter	Meg Long	Sally Smith
Sandy Casper	Gerry Mayes	Barbara Starling
Mildred Cella	Anne McCurdy	Angela Steely
Pam Clinton	Kathy McIver	Judy Stidham
Dail Cobb	Judy McKown	Mary Louise Symcox
Sharri Conway	Donna McMullan	Gina Thompson
Shelley Cox	Lynn McTeer	Betty Tindel
Maureen Crook	Betty Michael	Carol Toperzer
Jenny Dakil	Marcia Miller	Judy Travis
Claudia Davis	Carrie Mitchell	Pat Tubbs
Jan Dewbre	Gina Mitchell	Ellen Usry
Nancy Dill	John Moricoli	Annette Valentino
B. J. Dow	Mary Helen Moricoli	Susan Vassilakos
Janice Drummond	Gail Mullins	Carolyn Walden
Pat Ducray	Pat Murray	Carol Warner
Jennifer Elliott	Cassie Nash	Cammy Weaver
Julie England	Meg Newville	Pat Welch
Marsha Ferrier	Ann Niemeyer	Dianne Williams
Barbara Fineman	Glenna Ott	Candy Willis
Lolly Frank	Peggy Pappas	Elizabeth Windes
Mary Carol Gilbert	Helen Parker	Rachel Zelby
Ginger Gilmartin-Smith	Sharon Parker	
Patti Gipson	Risa Pierce	

Recipe Testers

The Cookbook Committee gratefully acknowledges the enormous commitment and contribution of those who tested all submitted recipes for *Tailgates to Tea Parties*. They generously gave their time and talents in order to select and perfect the recipes. Please accept our apologies if we have inadvertently excluded any recipe tester.

Dot Adkins	Lisa Gipson	Chris Purcell
Jerrie Anderson	Carolyn Glad	Nancy Pyle
Judith Anderson	Becky Heeney	Pat Richardson
Becky Archey	Sandra Hook	Beth Ridgway
Mignon Merchant Ball	Adele Hoving	Carolyn Rodgers
Jane Barrett	Donna Hughes	Lee Ann Rogers
Kathy Barrett	Marca January	Brenda Runkle
Mona Barringer	Dorothea Johnson	Jeri Saliba
Anita Bednar	Lori Kennedy	Jill Schaefer
Ruth Beller	Paula Kopecky	Carolyn Schmidt
Debbie Bugg	Jean Kugler	Jackie Shrode
Jennifer Bynum	Juli Lane	Judy Smith
Karla Campbell	Linda Leemaster	Sally Smith
Sue Carter	Dorothy Lilly	Sheri Straughn
Pam Clinton	Linda McCurdy	Mary Eve Summers
Dail Cobb	Denese McDonald	Janet Thomas
Mary Coleman	Judy McKown	Karrie Thompson
Dona Coulter	Liz McKown	Carol Toperzer
Doug Coulter	Donna McMullan	Judy Travis
Maureen Crook	Mary Helen Moricoli	Susan Vassilakos
Jenny Dakil	Gail Mullins	Pat Welch
Sheryl Dillard	Cassie Nash	Candy Willis
B. J. Dow	Ann Niemeyer	JoAnne Zmud
Jennifer Elliott	Glenna Ott	
Barbara Fineman	Helen Parker	
Mary Carol Gilbert	Janet Preble	

Photographers

KONRAD EEK

Konrad Eek received his Bachelor of Fine Arts degree from the University of Oklahoma in 1988. He has exhibited in numerous one-person and group shows, and his work appears in the permanent collection of the Fred Jones Memorial Art Museum and in the Midwest Photography Archives. For four years, he was the Production Manager of the Steven Michael Studios in Dallas, after which he was Director of Photography at PGI LLC in Oklahoma City for four years. He currently owns and operates Maxwell Eek Design Photography, a commercial photography studio in Norman, Oklahoma. The studio specializes in advertising and catalog photography. In addition to his commercial work, Konrad has a long-term commitment to arts education. He has taught advanced photography classes for Oklahoma City Community College for the last five years. He has also taught photography and darkroom technique to high school students and adults for the Oklahoma Arts Institute for more than a decade. Additionally, he is currently serving on the Arts Institute Board of Directors and their Visual Arts Advisory Panel.

SIMON HURST

Simon Hurst is a native of the south of England. He always had a love of the arts and wanted to become a painter. After picking up a camera in college, he realized his passion for life would be photography. He studied commercial photography and advertising in West Yorkshire, England, and graduated in 1995. After graduation, Simon took a position as a cruise ship photographer. He traveled to exotic places such as China, Australia, New Zealand, Indonesia, Japan, Russia, Alaska, and the Caribbean. It was in the Caribbean that Simon met his wife, Brina. Her home was Oklahoma, and after the toss of a coin, it was decided that they would live there. Simon worked as a freelance photographer and assistant until taking a full-time position at Shevaun Williams & Associates Commercial Photography in Norman, Oklahoma. Simon enjoys being associate photographer and studio manager at Shevaun Williams. Shooting everything from people to places to products, Simon's desire to create imagery is more than satisfied.

SHEVAUN WILLIAMS

It was a college summer session in Paris and the south of France that began this Oklahoma native's love affair with travel and the camera. "I loved the fresh perspectives gained through the lens," she says of her experiences with a borrowed 35mm camera. When she returned to the University of Oklahoma that fall, she pursued a curriculum in photography. Her client list includes J.C. Penney Corporation; Orlando, Florida's Fashion Square; Harold's Stores; Shepler's Western Wear; K. Kristopf Designs; County Seat; Aerobicwear of New York City; and the *New York Times*. Through her work with these clients, Shevaun has garnered numerous local, district, and national Ad Club awards, or "Addys." Her fine art is featured in The Guild Sourcebook, Altamira Galleries in New York; CP Interiors, Palm Beach Gardens, Florida; and LFA Art Management in Cambridge, Massachusetts. Most recently, she has partnered with Photo Japan to showcase her fine art images from Japan. Today, a 90-year-old, 4,500-square-foot historic downtown Norman building is home to Shevaun Williams & Associates, Commercial Photography Inc. The renovated space includes a full kitchen, makeup/dressing facilities, a staging area, four separate studio spaces, as well as galleries to display her fine art. She has served her clients with the highest quality product and dedicated customer service in a friendly atmosphere for over 15 years. She loves the dynamics of teamwork and the creative process. She continues to be inspired by the art of photography.

Index

187

190

Index

Tailgates to Tea Parties

Assistance League of Norman
809 Wall Street
Norman, Oklahoma 73069

Name
_____

Street Address
_____

City _____ State _____ Zip _____

Telephone
_____

YOUR ORDER	QUANTITY	TOTAL
Tailgates to Tea Parties at $24.95 per book		$
Oklahoma residents add 8% sales tax		$
Postage and handling at $3.00 per book		$
TOTAL		$

Method of Payment: [   ] American Express   [   ] MasterCard   [   ] VISA
[   ] Check(s) payable to Assistance League of Norman

Account Number _____   Expiration Date _____

Signature _____

Photocopies will be accepted.